Plasticity of Development

Plasticity of Development

edited by Steven E. Brauth, William S. Hall, and
Robert J. Dooling

A Bradford Book
The MIT Press
Cambridge, Massachusetts
London, England

This book was set in Palatino by the Maple-Vail Book Manufacturing Group and was
printed and bound in the United States of America.

Library of Congress Cataloging-in-Publication Data

Plasticity of development / edited by Steven E. Brauth, William S.
  Hall, Robert J. Dooling.
  p.   cm.
  Revised papers presented at a series of lectures, during the
  1986–87 academic year. Organized by the Program for Developmental
  Research, University of Maryland, College Park.
  "A Bradford book."
  Includes bibliographical references and index.
  ISBN 0-262-02326-1
  1. Nature and nurture—Congresses. 2. Developmental psychology—
  Congresses. 3. Psychology, Comparative—Congresses.
  4. Psycholinguistics—Congresses. I. Brauth, Steven E. II. Hall,
  William S. III. Dooling, Robert J. IV. University of Maryland,
  College Park. Program for Developmental Research.
  BF341.P53   1991
  155.2'34—dc20   90-26227
                                                                 CIP

Contents

Preface   vii

Acknowledgments   ix

Chapter 1
Introduction   1

Chapter 2
Continuity and Discontinuity in Development   11
Jerome Kagan

Chapter 3
Uptight and Laid-Back Monkeys: Individual Differences in the
Response to Social Challenges   27
Stephen J. Suomi

Chapter 4
Theoretical Issues in Investigating Intellectual Plasticity   57
Sandra Scarr

Chapter 5
Perception, Cognition, and the Ontogenetic and Phylogenetic
Emergence of Human Speech   73
Patricia J. Kuhl

Chapter 6
The Instinct for Vocal Learning: Songbirds   107
Peter Marler

Chapter 7
Plasticity of Cortical Development   127
Pasko Rakic

Chapter 8
Epilogue   163

Name Index   171
Subject Index   175

Errata

Plasticity of Development
Edited by Steven E. Brauth, William S. Hall, and Robert J. Dooling

The author of chapter 5 is Patricia K. Kuhl. In some places her name has been misprinted as Patricia J. Kuhl. Please accept our apologies for this error.

Preface

The nature-nurture issue has probably stimulated more empirical and theoretical work than any other issue in the field of psychology. This issue has come to the fore again with the rise in importance of cognitive science in psychology and the current interest in understanding the nature of self-organizing systems in the field of artificial intelligence. With this renewed interest have come fresh approaches and new insights in diverse fields including child psychology, animal learning, brain development, and psycholinguistics. To address this set of issues, the Program for Developmental Research at the University of Maryland, College Park, organized a series of lectures by distinguished speakers on the subject of developmental plasticity, presented during the 1986–87 academic year. The lectures were revised in 1990 and organized into a carefully edited volume providing state-of-the-art research results.

Jerome Kagan, Professor of Psychology, Harvard University, is internationally known for his work in child development. His research on continuity of development for anxiety and mitigation of anxiety has received critical acclaim in both scientific and lay publications. Stephen Suomi, NIMH Primate Laboratory, has continued research begun in collaboration with Harry Harlow and has extended this research into new fields, including the psychopharmacology of behavioral development. His work on continuity of social development parallels that of Kagan in many respects. Sandra Scarr, Commonwealth Professor of Psychology at the University of Virginia, is well known for her pathbreaking work on behavioral genetics and children's intellectual development.

Peter Marler, Professor at the University of California, Davis, is considered by many to be the key figure in establishing the birdsong model in neuroethology. He is the recipient of many awards and honors in the field of animal behavior. Patricia J. Kuhl, Professor of Hearing and Speech Sciences at the University of Washington, has concentrated on the field of human speech development. Her research on perceptual and motor processes in child speech development has provided new insights into phenomena such as categorical perception and motor learning.

Pasko Rakic, Professor and Chair, Section on Neuroanatomy, Yale University School of Medicine, works in the field of developmental neurobiology. He discovered and described the role of radial glial cells in cortical morphogenesis and recently has shown that competition and cell death in the embryo act as mechanisms for shaping cortical growth and development.

Steven E. Brauth, William S. Hall, and Robert J. Dooling of the Department of Psychology at the University of Maryland, College Park, are editors of the volume. Brauth is a comparative neuroanatomist, whose research includes studies of brain evolution in vertebrates and development of the auditory system in psittacine birds. Hall is a researcher in the field of developmental psychology, whose work on child language use and development has been aimed particularly at understanding the development of metacognition. Dooling is a Comparative Psychologist who works on vocal learning and audition in birds.

Acknowledgments

The lectures and the preparation of this manuscript were supported by the College of Behavioral and Social Sciences and the Department of Psychology at the University of Maryland, College Park. We gratefully acknowledge this support. Special acknowledgment is due to Patricia Walker, Thomas J. Park, Susan Brown, Michael Blair, and Kazuo Okanoya, who assisted with the recording of the lectures. The lectures and this volume would not have been possible without their help. A special note of thanks is also due to Randi Dutch, manager of the Rossborough Inn, who provided the gracious setting in which the lectures were given.

Plasticity of Development

Chapter 1
Introduction

In a now classic series of writings, Waddington (1957, 1960, 1962, 1968a, 1968b) elucidated the properties of what he called the *epigenetic system* in order to explain how phenotypic characteristics arise during development through a complex series of interactions between genetic programs and environmental signals. In referring to these processes as epigenetic, Waddington meant to say that environmental signals act *upon* the genome in order to bring about the expression of all of the morphological and behavioral characteristics displayed by individual organisms at different points during the life span. Some aspects of these programs are tightly constrained, species-typical processes that tend to produce important aspects of the phenotype even in abnormal environments. Waddington (1960) referred to these processes as *strongly canalized*. Other epigenetic processes are less tightly constrained and provide the basis for phenotypic characteristics that show substantial individual variation among members of the same species.

The strongly canalized characteristics of any species are presumably those that are crucial for fitness (i.e., for survival and reproduction of genes). As such, identification of the mechanisms of canalization provides insights into the nature of speciation. On the other hand, study of the development of the more weakly canalized features of the phenotype provides insight into normal patterns of phenotypic variation within a species. Both are essential for understanding the nature of the biological basis of developmental plasticity.

Viewed in this way, the study of plasticity of development focuses on elucidating the cause-effect sequences underlying epigenesis. Such studies provide a platform for addressing fundamental questions in biology and psychology related to both the *proximate* and *ultimate* causal sequences underlying plasticity of development.

Proximate causal sequences are the immediate cause-effect sequences by which information in the genotype is "read out" during development in the presence of environmental stimuli. Explication of proximate causal sequences is important because it allows us to determine *how* the organism develops in a particular range of environments.

For example, Pasko Rakic describes the ontogenetic processes that produce the primate cerebral cortex. The cerebral cortex is the organ of higher cognitive functions including perception, thought, memory, and judgment. As such, it provides the neural basis for functions that are critically important for fitness. As might be expected, the anatomical organization of the cortex is extraordinarily complex, presumably reflecting the complexity of the behaviors it supports, which raises the question of how this highly adaptive circuitry emerges during embryonic life. As described by Rakic, there is normally remarkably little variation in the basic patterns of neurogenesis, migration of neuroblasts, and subsequent patterns of neuronal interconnections among members of the same species. Yet these patterns of neuronal connectivity in the cortex can be changed, and striking plasticity unmasked, when experimenters alter the environment of the developing embryo. These studies provide insights into how the "wiring diagram" of the brain is implemented during development and provide clues about the nature of the epigenetic processes that canalize the development of cortical circuitry in primates.

Ultimate causal sequences, on the other hand, refer to the nature of the *selection pressures* that enable certain individuals expressing particular genetically based phenotypic characteristics during their lifetime to leave more offspring (or project more copies of their genes) than other members of their species exhibiting quantitatively or qualitatively different phenotypic characteristics at comparable points in the life span. Such questions concern *why* particular character traits arise during development in a particular spatio-temporal pattern and provide explanations about the adaptive significance of these traits.

For example, Peter Marler points out that although oscine songbirds rely on learning to develop species-specific vocalizations, these learning processes are both constrained and facilitated by genetic programs. This is important because song plays a crucial role in coordinating social and reproductive behavior and in some cases maintains a degree of geographical isolation among breeding populations. Thus the "instinct to learn," as Marler puts it, is an essential ingredient in speciation. Marler's work on bird song not only provides intriguing models for studying canalized learning systems but also puts these phenomena in the context of the natural history and evolutionary biology of these species. As a result it provides insight into both the proximate and ultimate causal sequences underlying developmental plasticity for one kind of complex behavior (vocal learning) in an important group of animals.

The Comparative Approach in Developmental Biopsychology

The approach taken in this book is therefore the *comparative* approach. For the comparative psychologist, development is viewed not only in terms of specific ontogenetic mechanisms (proximate causal sequences) but also in terms of the ultimate causal sequences by which such epigenetic programs came about. Such studies address the most fundamental issues in biology and psychology, providing a platform not only for studying the mechanisms of individual development but for understanding the adaptive significance of developmental pathways as well.

Figure 1.1 provides a schematic representation of the relationships between proximate and ultimate causal sequences and developmental processes. In essence it focuses attention on the fact that the genetic program's code for developmental processes is contingent on appropriate environmental stimulation. The genetic programs themselves result from differential reproductive success of individuals carrying particular phenotypes (i.e., from natural selection). The expression of these genetic programs therefore depends upon the presence of appropriate environmental signals, which were presumably also present in the environments in which evolution of the species occurred.

Three fundamental problems in developmental biopsychology are suggested: (1) Is there *continuity* in development, i.e., what is the nature of the epigenetic programs unfolding at each phase of development? (2) What is the nature of the *biological and environmental signals,* i.e., what are the signals associated with each of these epigenetic processes? (3) What is the *adaptive significance* of these ontogenetic programs, i.e., how do the resulting phenotypes enable individuals to reproduce their genes in the environments in which they develop?

Contemporary Issues in Developmental Biopsychology

In this volume six contemporary scientists present their research into the nature of epigenetic processes. Three of these research programs (Suomi, Marler, and Rakic) primarily or exclusively involve the study of nonhuman species, while three (Kagan, Scarr, and Kuhl) primarily or exclusively investigate epigenetic processes in human development. Each author addresses one or more of these broad questions concerning the nature of epigenetic systems that produce behavioral and morphological phenotypes.

The first question, concerning *continuity* in developmental processes, is addressed by Kagan (chapter 2) and Suomi (chapter 3). Ka-

→ Proximate Causal Sequences →

GENOTYPE → EPIGENESIS → PHENOTYPE

Contains a set of instructions for producing the organism in a range of environments.

Embryonic and post-embryonic development is a canalized process involving a set of interactions between biological signals and environmental cues.

Morphological and behavioral characteristics of the individual.

← Ultimate Causal Sequences ←

SELECTION

Differential Gene Replication Due to Genetically Based Phenotypic Differences.

Figure 1.1
A schematic diagram indicating the relationships between proximate and ultimate causal sequences in epigenesis as currently understood in developmental biopsychology.

gan begins by pointing out that many developmental processes act as enabling mechanisms during specific points in ontogeny and essentially cease to function at the end of such periods. In effect, these programs enable the developing phenotype to reach intermediate targets, or transitional stages, at which point different epigenetic programs become active. This has great significance for the psychologist interested in studying intellectual and personality development because it raises the following question: Do adult personality characteristics appear early in childhood, or do childhood behavioral characteristics represent, essentially, temporary predispositions that do not, by themselves, predict adult character traits?

For at least one important personality characteristic, response to challenge and stress, the answer appears to be that there is indeed continuity. As described by Kagan, characteristic behavioral responses to social fear and anxiety-producing situations such as separations appear early in infancy. Although the specific behaviors expressed in such situations change over the lifetime, the occurrence of these types of behaviors within individuals is remarkably stable and predictable across the entire life span. Furthermore, these behavioral characteristics have well-defined physiological correlates, including cardiac response patterns, that show striking consistency within individuals across the life span. Although anxious children can learn coping strategies for mitigating the effects of stress and social fear, the associated physiological responses are not changed by these coping strategies and persist into adulthood. Thus this research also provides insights into the second question concerning the nature of *biological and environmental* factors guiding epigenesis.

Steve Suomi describes virtually the same phenomenon in Rhesus monkeys. The behaviors and physiological correlates of rhesus monkeys are so similar to those of human children described by Kagan (chapter 2), that it seems almost inescapable to conclude that at least some of these behaviors are homologous (derived from a common ancestor). In addition to demonstrating striking consistency across the life span of individual rhesus monkeys, Suomi uses cross-fostering studies to show that a suite of behavioral characteristics related to how the animals mitigate anxiety and social fear possesses a strong biological base. Cardiac responses, adrenocortical output, a neurotransmitter turnover in the central nervous system can all be predicted from individual behavioral response data. Suomi's research thus also provides insights into the biological underpinnings of these developmental processes.

This result does not mean that early influences, particularly characteristics of the mother, have no consequences for the developing individual. On the contrary, infants reared by more nurturant monkey mothers have a better chance of establishing valuable social relationships with adults later and apparently of establishing dominance within their own social groups. Thus Suomi's work not only helps to unravel the roles of biological and social environmental factors in the development of adult personality characteristics but also provides insights into the impact of these characteristics on social success (i.e., fitness) and therefore sheds light on the third question concerning the *adaptive significance* of epigenetic programs.

Sandra Scarr (chapter 4) deals with the problem of continuity within development in human children and investigates specifically the role of adoption and home environment on the development of these characteristics. The results show that although there is some correlation between IQ test scores and personality characteristics for adopted children and parents early in the children's lives, these correlations fall to zero as the children reach puberty and adulthood. Perhaps even more mysterious is the finding that intellectual and personality characteristics for biological siblings, including fraternal twins, become increasingly *dissimilar* as the children mature, while those of biological twins become even more similar.

Scarr explains the data in terms of epigenetic processes. Drawing on her own work as well as the work of other developmental psychologists, Scarr points out that children both *select* and *elicit* the environmental signals guiding development. Although the home environment seems to exert a global effect on the development of intellectual and personality characteristics, to a surprising extent children create the environmental niches they fill. Furthermore, the home environment itself is a product of the behaviors of the parents, and these behaviors have a substantial genetic component. Thus for children raised by biological parents both the children's genetic endowment and their environment are highly correlated with the parents' genotypes.

Scarr's work provides insights into the nature of the actual environmental signals controlling intellectual development. It thus addresses the second question concerning the nature of *biological* and *environmental* signals guiding epigenesis, as well as the first (i.e., continuity). Additional insight into the nature of the biological and environmental signals controlling epigenetic programs is provided by the work of Pat Kuhl concerning the development of speech perception in human children.

There is overwhelming evidence that language learning in humans depends on innate predispositions and therefore can be properly regarded as a canalized process (Fishbein 1976). The pioneering studies of Lenneberg (1967) showed clearly that language acquisition in children of normal intelligence can be characterized in terms of predictable learning phases, which are accomplished in essentially the same order, although not necessarily to completion, by retarded children. Chomsky (1969) and other linguists have argued in favor of the existence of an innate language acquisition system (see also Lightfoot 1983). Thus the case for biological preparedness in human language learning is very strong.

Despite strong agreement among linguists and developmental psychologists that language learning involves innate predispositions, there is much less certainty concerning the nature of the learning mechanisms involved. Clearly an interrelated set of innate predispositions must exist, directing the child's attention to human speech sounds and providing both the motivation and capacity to express complex thoughts verbally. Human children from infancy (if not earlier) appear attentive to both the rhythm and sounds of human speech and preferentially imitate human speech sounds rather than the sounds of animals or other environmental noises. Later they spontaneously ask questions about people and objects in their environments and develop grammatical competence even without specific instruction on the part of caretakers or peers (Newport 1977; Newport et al. 1977).

Kuhl's work provides insights into the nature of some of these predispositions. As she describes in this volume, children not only pay close attention to human speech sounds, but they also appear to be innately prepared to associate the sound of utterances with facial gestures correlated with their production. One can see that this would probably facilitate language acquisition by focusing and maintaining the child's attention on the source of specific utterances in dyadic interactions.

Kuhl also applies the *comparative approach* to the study of speech perception with interesting results. It is well known that human observers do not perceive graded changes in voice onset time (VOT) in a continuous manner. This phenomenon, called categorical perception, is hypothesized to underlie a number of speech-sound contrasts. It has also been taken to represent evidence of innate preparedness for speech perception and language development in humans. Kuhl's review tempers this conclusion by showing that nonhuman animals are also sensitive to these speech-sound contrasts and respond in the same way as human observers. The use of the comparative approach, therefore, provides evidence that these perceptual discontinuities are the result of general auditory mechanisms common to humans and to some other animals, they do not represent a special speech perception mechanism in humans. The challenge is to determine what is general and what is special in human speech perception and language development. This issue bears directly on the question of the "open" versus "closed" learning systems described by Marler (chapter 6) for song learning in oscine species.

Comparative research, such as that described by Marler and Kuhl, can provide valuable clues about the nature of biological mechanisms in learning. There are striking parallels between the kinds of innate predispositions to attend to and learn human speech sounds described by Kuhl in human children and the "instinct to learn" in oscine songbirds described by Marler (chapter 6). Such predispositions ensure that learning follows a predictable course while remaining at least partially open and malleable in response to changes in environmental stimulation. Thus study of these kinds of learning processes can provide insights into the nature of canalization mechanisms.

For example, in many oscine species individuals selectively attend to and learn songs produced only by other members of their species, thus indicating a preference for a particular domain of acoustic signals. In contrast, other species show less innate preferences, yet follow a predictable path for learning songs. Clearly the path of song development is shaped by multiple factors, the relative contributions of which may vary substantially between even closely related species.

The most detailed account of the *biological* and *environmental* signals controlling epigenesis in this volume is Rakic's work (chapter 7) on cerebral cortical development in primates. Although a highly predictable, species-typical pattern of neuroanatomical connections emerges in embryonic life, this pattern of neuronal connectivity is not established entirely through a genetically coded plan. Instead, early in embryonic life there is a vast overproduction of neurons, many of which establish incorrect connections with other neurons. Through competitive processes in which neurons establishing correct (species-typical) connections persist while others die, the species-typical pattern of cortical circuitry emerges.

In addition to providing insights into biological and environmental signals controlling cortical ontogeny, Rakic's work provides evidence for the theory that epigenetic mechanisms may have played a role in the evolution of neural circuits. This is because changes in any part of a neural circuit (hypertrophy, rearrangement of neurons, etc.) resulting from changes in the genome (the effects of mutations, etc.) would necessarily entail changes in other neuronal populations that are part of the same circuits as a result of epigenesis. For example, Rakic shows that disruption of the development of the primary geniculo-striate visual pathway leads to reorganization of portions of the parietal lobes during development, presumably because ectopic projections, which normally would have disappeared during embryonic life, persist due to reduced competition.

Significance

Taken together, the research described here represents some of the most innovative in the field of developmental biopsychology. These studies address important issues, including continuity of developmental processes, the nature of biological and environmental signals controlling epigenetic mechanisms, and the adaptive significance of developmental pathways. The comparative approach is explicit in some research, such as Suomi's (chapter 3), Kuhl's (chapter 5), Marler's (chapter 6) and Rakic's (chapter 7). In some of these cases (Suomi, Rakic) the processes described presumably correspond to homologous processes in humans.

In addition to providing model systems based on the study of homologous adaptations in nonhuman species, comparative research can identify similar phenotypic patterns arising due to *homoplasy*. Homoplastic adaptations are the result of parallel or convergent evolution and are particularly interesting because they provide ways to test theories about the adaptive significance of phenotypic characters (Northcutt 1984). For example, striking similarities between song learning in oscine species and vocal learning in human children reflect the occurrence of homoplasy. The existence of similar adaptations in disparate species suggests that there are constraints on the range of possible neural mechanisms that can serve such behavioral functions. Marler discusses these possibilities, as well as the general usefulness of animal communication systems, as models for understanding basic biological principles in socialization and learning.

It is tempting to speculate that the field of developmental biopsychology is on the threshold of a more comprehensive synthesis in which the results of studies by comparative psychologists, developmental psychologists, and neurobiologists form an interrelated body of knowledge sharing a common theory. This prospect is particularly exciting in view of the explosive growth of knowledge in the neurosciences and the possibilities this growth raises for enhancing our understanding of developmental mechanisms at the cellular and neural systems levels.

References

Chomsky, N. (1969). *Acquisition of syntax in children from 5 to 10*. Cambridge: MIT Press.

Fishbein, H. D. (1976). *Evolution, development and children's learning*. Pacific Palisades: Goodyear Publishing

Lenneberg, E. H. (1967). *Biological Foundations of Language*. New York: John Wiley & Sons.

Lightfoot, D. (1983). *The language lottery: Toward a biology of grammar*. Cambridge: MIT Press.

Newport, E. L. (1977). Motherese: The speech of mothers to young children. In *Cognitive theory*, Vol. 2, ed. N. J. Castellan, D. B. Pisoni and G. R. Potts. Hillsdale, N.J.: Lawrence Erlbaum Associates.

Newport, E. L., Gleitman. H., and Gleitman, L. R. (1977). Mother, I'd rather do it myself: Some effects and non-effects of maternal speech style. In *Talking to children: Language input and acquisition*, ed. C. Snow and C. Ferguson. Cambridge: Cambridge University Press.

Northcutt, R. G. (1984). Evolution of the vertebrate central nervous system: Patterns and processes. *American Zoologist* 24:701–716.

Waddington, C. H. (1957). *The strategy of genes: The discussion of aspects of theoretical biology*. London: Allan & Unwin.

Waddington, C. H. (1960). Genetic assimilation. In *Advances in Genetics*, ed. E. W. Caspari and J. W. Thoday. New York: Academic Press.

Waddington, C. H. (1962). *New patterns in genetics and development*. New York: Columbia University Press.

Waddington, C. H. (1968a). The theory of evolution today. In *Beyond reductionism*, ed. A. Koestler and J. R. Smythies. New York: Macmillan.

Waddington, C. H. (1968b). The basic ideas of biology. In *Towards a theoretical biology*. *I. Prologomena*. Birmingham: The Kynoch Press.

Chapter 2

Continuity and Discontinuity in Development

Jerome Kagan

Every scientific discipline is characterized by a series of complementary themata; when disciplines reach maturity, investigators recognize that they must accommodate to the complementary themes. A clear illustration is seen in evolutionary theory. For the first few decades after Darwin's book biologists assumed that natural selection was the only force in evolution. When the gene was postulated, there was a brief period at the turn of the century when natural selection was dismissed, and biologists assumed that mutation could explain all of evolution. Today we accept the modern synthesis and realize that both genes and natural selection contribute to evolution.

Among psychologists nature and nurture constitute an important pair of complementary themes. Most psychologists now acknowledge that these two forces exist in a complementary relation to each other. Continuity and discontinuity represent another pair of themata in development. Although we can find examples of both in ontogeny, I begin by asking why it is that Western scholars discussing human nature have resisted acknowledging discontinuities, even though biologists recognize discontinuities in evolution and historians appreciate that many events have short prologues. But in most textbooks the development of the child is usually described in the following prototypic sentence: "New structures grow gradually out of old ones and retain some of the old."

This premise leads investigators to regard human development as a detective story. One notes an action in an infant and must figure out what phenomenon might be its derivative at a later age. Starkey and his colleagues (1983) published a paper on the concept of number in infants. Because 5-year-olds have a clear concept of number, it was assumed that one should see its origins in infancy. William Stern (1930) wrote that the babbling of a one-month-old represented the origin of later speech. Other nineteenth-century observers noted that if one

This research was supported in part by the John D. and Catherine T. MacArthur Foundation.

wanted to see the origin of the adult proprietary instinct, one would place a small pencil in the palm of a newborn infant and see how it grasped the object.

It is so easy for anyone of average intelligence to detect an element of similarity between a quality in an infant and a quality in an adult that it is not particularly creative to imagine that a particular infant behavior will become aggression, dependency, or anxiety. Havelock Ellis (1900) suggested that there was a similarity between a nursing infant and adult sexual intercourse, noting that the erectile nipple corresponded to the erectile penis, the watery mouth of the infant to the vagina, and the vitally albuminous milk to the vitally albuminous semen. He believed that the satisfaction of mother and child in the transfer from one to the other of a precious organized fluid is the one true physiological analogy to the relation of a man and a woman.

Although many readers may smile at that analogy, Freud and many of his colleagues did not. Today we take seriously the idea that the origin of a love relationship in adults is the trust relationship between an infant and its mother. I believe this analogy rests on a base as weak as the one that Ellis imagined.

We must view many of the phenomena of early development as temporary adaptations. When a young chick hatches from an egg, the motor responses the bird makes occur once and only once. The bird will never make those particular responses again. Similarly the cry of a 7-month-old child in the presence of a stranger, which is universal, is an ontogenetic adaptation. When I was younger, however, I thought that the anxiety toward a stranger was the early form of fear of failure or conflict in the older child. I believe that Bowlby (1969) made the same error when he likened the anxiety seen at separation in the one-year-old to the mourning of wives and sweethearts when their husbands did not come home from war.

The deep belief that these continuities exist, combined with our ability to pick out similarities, has led many psychologists and parents to assume that the basic responses and emotions established during the first two years of life will be preserved indefinitely.

Let us review the evidence for this belief. Moss and Sussman (1980) have reviewed much of this literature in their chapter "Change and Continuity in Development," edited by Orville Brim and myself. The answer to the question of continuity will depend on what psychological unit is being studied. Remember that children possess schemata, memories, and feelings as well as actions. However, over 99 percent of the research on the stability of human characteristics has quantified overt behavior because social scientists do not know how to measure the continuity of emotions. Similarly we do not know how to measure the schemata a one-year-old might have acquired. Thus psychologists do what empiricists would do: they evaluate what can be measured. When investigators focus on behaviors such as dependency, aggression, and irritability, then most of the longitudinal studies are in general agreement that until 5 or 6 years of age it is very difficult to find preservation of individual differences in the child. In the Fels study most of the behaviors did not begin to show long-term stability until the child was 6 or 7 years of age (Kagan and Moss 1962). Similar results were found in the longitudinal study at the University of California. A similar result holds for children who have grown up with some stress during childhood (Rathburn, DiVigilo, and Waldfogel 1958). After the Second World War some young children were adopted by upper-middle-class families on the East Coast. These infants were visited by a team led by Samuel Waldfogel, a psychoanalyst. This group of investigators believed in continuities and found them during the first few months because the children were anxious and clung to their new parents. However, a few years later all symptoms were gone, and the children appeared well adapted to their new settings. At the end of their 1958 paper in the *American Journal of Orthopsychiatry* they noted that their original premises were flawed.

Almost 20 years later Winick, Myers, and Harris (1975) found Korean orphans who had been adopted by middle-class West Coast families. When they evaluated these children a year later when they were in the sixth grade, they discovered that their IQ scores were normal and that there was no case of learning disability in the group. The animal literature also supports discontinuity. In a review of the literature Cairns and Hood (1983) noted that even for animals raised in the laboratory there was not much preservation of behavioral qualities from infancy to reproductive maturity.

Moreover, even after 6 years of age the magnitudes of the correlations reflecting preservation of qualities such as academic ability, aggressivity, or dependency are only about 0.3. Olweus (1981) believes that I am too harsh in my conclusions about continuity. However, the rank order stability for aggressive behavior from age 6 through age 20 is only on the order of 0.3. There is some continuity, but it does not hit you between the eyes.

There is therefore a great deal of plasticity in development with respect to behavior. If this is true, why do we continue to be loyal to the idea of continuity? I would like to suggest at least four reasons why so many psychologists are biased toward continuity. First, America is still a Puritan nation. I use the word Puritan in its original sense. Most Americans want to believe that there is a purpose to their lives, that there is something each of us can do that will affect the future.

That is one reason why we urge all mothers to make a serious investment of love and care in their infant. We would not do so if these behaviors had no future consequences. Second, the belief in preservation is mechanistic. It is assumed that a structure learned in infancy will be incorporated into a later structure. A life is treated very much like building a house according to a plan. There are no occult forces, no unpredictable events that will disrupt the orderly chain of development.

A third factor rests with our language. In many languages of the world, including languages in the Pacific and the Far East, one does not apply a name for an infant quality to an adult. The word *intelligent* or *angry* applied to an adult would not be applied to an infant. In certain parts of Melanesia there is a word *fago*, which means compassion, but one never applies that word to a child under six years of age. In English, however, words such as *intelligent, labile, irritable, angry, joyful, happy, sad,* and *depressed* are applied to both infants and adults. The implication is that the depression we note in a 40-year-old man who has lost his wife also applies to a one-year-old. The fact that we use the same words tempts us to believe that we are talking about the same property.

Perhaps the most important basis for the belief in continuity is the commitment to political egalitarianism. Most Americans want to believe that it is possible to have a society in which all people are relatively equal in dignity and financial security. However, when we look at 5-year-olds, we see that is not possible, for the differences among 5-year-olds coming from lower- or middle-class homes are extraordinary. Because we want to believe that the egalitarian goal can be reached, it is necessary to believe that if all parents acted properly during the first five years of life, we could attain our political ideal. That desire is so strong, it continues to search for its validation.

I should now like to present some data indicating evidence of some discontinuities in development. These discontinuities refer to behaviors that emerge because of maturation of the brain. I do not believe these structures have been growing gradually.

I start with recall memory. We studied children longitudinally from 7 through 12 months of age using the standard object permanence situation. There are two covers, and an object is hidden under one of them with delays of one, three, or seven seconds and either a transparent or opaque screen separating the child from the examiner during the delay. Each child was seen once each month. The ability to remember the location of the hidden toy over increasing delays improved with age. By 14 months every child solved this problem with an opaque screen for an interval of seven seconds. Thus, there is a dramatic increase in recall memory across the second half of the first year. Adele Diamond, who is now at the University of Pennsylvania, did a similar study with a longitudinal sample of infants. These infants were administered the A not B problems, and she found the delay at each age at which the child would fail to make the A not B error. She then increased the delay to produce the error. With age, the child tolerated a longer delay without making the error. Even though the 9-month-old children were familiar with the problem, if the delay between the hiding and allowing them to reach was too long, they made the error (Diamond 1983).

The period between 8 and 12 months, when memory is maturing, is also the time when stranger and separation fears appear. Infants from many different settings, including a barrio in Antigua, Guatemala, Israeli Kibbutzim, and the Kalahari Desert, were studied. Infants under eight months did not cry when their mother left them, but a large proportion of infants between 12 and 15 months of age did cry.

My interpretation of this fact is that separation fear cannot occur until the child's recall memory has matured. When a mother leaves a 6-month-old, the infant cannot retrieve the fact that she was present moments earlier and, therefore, has no cognitive dissonance to resolve. A 12-month-old can retrieve the schema of her former presence and compare that schema with the present on the stage of short-term memory. This infant has a problem—the mother was present earlier but is not present now. That inconsistency creates uncertainty and may lead the baby to cry.

Using inanimate objects, William Mason (1978) and his colleagues raised infant monkeys without contingent interaction. He placed these monkeys in novel environments on a regular schedule. Peak distress vocalizations and high heart rates occurred at about 130 days of age. Because the monkey's nervous system grows at a rate of about 3.5 to 4 times that of the infant, 130 days in an infant monkey is comparable to about 15 months in the human infant. That is the age when separation anxiety is most likely to occur in humans. The monkeys were not gradually becoming more anxious over the first four months. Rather, when certain nervous system connections were completed, the animal became capable of a new response; in this case anxiety to the novel situation. Thus, stranger and separation anxieties appear rather suddenly due to maturation of the brain.

During the last months of the second year another discontinuous set of behaviors occurs. For example, empathy now appears for the first time. Radke-Yarrow and her colleagues (Cummings, Zahn-Waxler, and Radke-Yarrow 1981) have written that this is a time when young children show empathy when they see someone hurt or distressed. In addition, the child will now refer to self for the first time. Laura Petitto (1983) studied deaf children of deaf parents who were learning sign language. These children first made the sign referring to self around 17 or 18 months of age, which is the time when hearing children make their first vocal references to self.

This is also the period when children show their first sense of right and wrong. A child is playing happily on a carpet. The mother is present, and a familiar examiner sits besides the child and asks if she can play. The examiner then models three acts. She might make the baby feed a doll or make some animals walk—acts that are comprehensible but difficult to remember and to implement. The examiner then says it is now the child's turn to play. She never says, Do what I did. In longitudinal and cross-sectional samples in the United States, as well as in cross-sectional samples of Fijian children, no child under 16 months cried to that request. But after 16 months, and reaching a peak at 20 to 21 months, the children became increasingly likely to cry when the examiner said it was their turn to play. I take this to mean this is a time when children are aware that they should imitate the examiner. That is, they have a sense of obligation but are unable to meet it. I suggest that this competence has not been growing gradually since the time the baby was one month old but is a discontinuity in development (Kagan 1981).

Up to now I have been presenting some examples of discontinuities in development. I now present a brief summary of our recent work on temperament, which suggests that there may be some continuities.

Temperament

The word temperament is used by most, but not all, psychologists to refer to the psychological qualities of infants that have considerable variation and, in addition, have a relatively, but not indefinitely, stable biological basis in the organism's genotype, even though different phenotypes emerge as the child grows. I believe that some of the temperamental differences among children are analogous to selected behavioral differences among closely related strains of monkeys.

The temperamental qualities that are most obvious to contemporary parents, and investigated most often by psychologists, include irritability, smiling, motor activity, and adaptability to new situations. These qualities are popular because they have implications for the ease with which parents can socialize their infant. It is not clear at the moment how many temperamental qualities will be discovered; it will certainly be more than 6, but we hope it will be less than 60. We will have to wait for history's answer.

Inhibited and Uninhibited Children

Steven Reznick, Nancy Snidman, and I, together with Cynthia Garcia-Coll, Wendy Coster, Michele Gersten, and many others in our laboratory, have been studying two complementary members from the large set of temperamental qualities (Kagan, Reznick, and Snidman 1988; Kagan 1989). The original behavioral referent for these qualities was the profile of 21- or 31-month-old children in a variety of unfamiliar situations. One of the few stable behavioral differences among children that is not correlated with social class or cognitive abilities is their initial reaction to unfamiliar situations for which they do not have an immediate coping reaction. Some children consistently became quiet, vigilant, and affectively subdued for a period of time. Others act with spontaneity, as though the distinctions between familiar and novel were of minimal psychological consequences. The situations that reveal these two qualities most often in young children between 2 and 4 years of age are encounters with unfamiliar children or adults, perhaps because the presence of unfamiliar people is a frequent basis for categorizing a setting as unfamiliar. Of course, it is rare to find a large number of children who are either consistently shy and affectively restrained or outgoing and spontaneous regardless of the social context. There is, however, a small group of children—we estimate it to be about 10 to 15 percent—who usually bring one or the other of these behavioral styles to unfamiliar situations. We call the shy children *inhibited* and the sociable children *uninhibited.*

We selected from large samples of Caucasian children, 21 months of age for cohort 1 and 31 months for cohort 2, those children who were either consistently shy, timid and fearful—inhibited—or sociable, bold, and fearless—uninhibited—when they encountered unfamiliar people or objects in our unfamiliar laboratory rooms. We had to screen by telephone and observe over 400 children in order to find 54 consistently inhibited and 53 consistently uninhibited children—about 15 percent of the children screened—with equal number of boys and girls in each group. These children were seen on three additional occasions; at the last assessment, at 7½ years of age, there were 41 children in each of the two cohorts—a loss of about 20 percent of the original sample.

On each of the assessments the children were observed in different situations. Usually the assessments included a testing session with a female examiner and, on a different day, a play situation with an unfamiliar child of the same age and sex. Details of the procedures can be found in our published papers (see Garcia-Coll et al. 1984; Kagan et al 1987; Reznick et al. 1986). We computed aggregate indexes of inhibition at each age, based on the child's tendency to be quiet and emotionally subdued during the test session with the examiner and socially avoidant with the unfamiliar children. At 5½ years of age the aggregate index included observations of the child's behavior in his or her school setting (Gersten 1986).

The indexes of inhibition and lack of inhibition at 7½ years were based on behavior in two laboratory situations. The first was a play situation involving seven to ten unfamiliar children of the same age and sex. Approximately 50 minutes of the session was devoted to structured, competitive games and about 30 minutes to unstructured free play interposed between each of the games. The two critical variables were number of spontaneous comments to the other children or supervising adults and proportion of time spent standing or playing apart from any other child in the room during the free-play intervals.

The second assessment context was an individual testing session with an unfamiliar female examiner who did not know the child's prior status. The two critical variables were latency to the sixth spontaneous comment to the examiner and the total number of spontaneous comments over the 90-minute session. The aggregate index of inhibition represented the average standard scores for the indexes from the two assessment situations. The intercoder reliabilities for those behavioral variables coded from videotapes were about 0.90.

Preserveration of Behavior

There was moderate preservation of the inhibited and uninhibited behavioral styles from the first assessments, at either 21 or 31 months, through 7½ years of age. The correlation between the original index of inhibition at 21 months and the aggregate index at 7½ years was +.67 ($p<.001$) for cohort 1 and +.39 ($p<.01$) for cohort 2. About three-fourths of the children in each cohort related their expected classification; that is, their standard score on the aggregate index at 7½ years was positive if they had been inhibited and negative if they had been uninhibited originally. Thus, the children who were most extreme initially were most likely to maintain their behavioral style. Although one-half of the original group of inhibited children from both cohorts no longer displayed an extreme degree of shyness, most of these children (80 percent) had still not acquired the unusually spontaneous demeanor characteristic of the typical uninhibited child.

A smaller number—about 10 percent—of uninhibited children became shy at 7½ years of age.

About three-fourths of the inhibited 7½-year-olds, compared with only one-fourth of the uninhibited children, had one or more unusual fears; for example, speaking voluntarily in the classroom, attending summer camp, remaining alone in the home, taking out the rubbish at night, or going to their bedroom alone in the evening. Further, one-third of the siblings of the inhibited children but not one sibling of an uninhibited child had one or more of these unusual fears. Finally, as Sheldon (1940) might have predicted, more of the inhibited children were of ectomorphic body build, while more uninhibited children were mesomorphic.

Several recent independent studies of monozygotic and dizygotic twins have found heritability of inhibited and uninhibited behavior. Adam Matheny (1989) of the University of Louisville studied 33 pairs of monozygotic and 32 pairs of dizygotic twins at 12, 18, 24, and 30 months. The intraclass correlation for an aggregate index of inhibition at each age ranged from 0.7 to 0.9 for the monozygotic twins and from 0.00 to 0.20 for the dizygotic twins. In addition, a research team at the Institute of Behavioral Genetics at the University of Colorado, which is conducting an extensive twin study, is finding significant heritability for inhibited and uninhibited behavior in 14- and 20-month-old children.

It is of interest that the most important finding from the study of the Fels longitudinal population, published in the book *Birth and Maturity* (Kagan and Moss 1962), was that the only psychological quality preserved from the first three years of life through adulthood was the characteristic we now call behavioral inhibition. A small group of children who were very fearful and timid during the first six years of life—about 15 percent of the total sample—retained that quality through adulthood, and these introverted men had a very stable heart rate under laboratory conditions. I shall return to this unexpected association later.

In a later collaboration with Richard Kearsley and Phillip Zelazo, we enrolled Chinese-American and Caucasian infants from similar social class backgrounds in a longitudinal study of the effect of day care across the period from 3 to 29 months of age. We found that although the effect of day care was minimal, the Chinese infants, whether attending our day-care center or raised only at home, were, relative to the Caucasians, more subdued, shy, and fearful and cried more intensely when their mother left them for a brief separation. They also had more stable heart rates than the Caucasian children (Kagan, Kearsley, and Zelazo 1978).

Types or a Continuum?

It is important to note that our results on the two longitudinal cohorts hold for children who had been selected to be extreme on shyness and sociability. However, because some investigators believe that these qualities form a continuum, it is important to determine whether these two groups of children lie on a continuum of sociability or whether they represent two qualitative types. During this century behavioral scientists who study behavior, thought, and emotion have favored continual over categories and linear over nonlinear relations. These suppositions dominate the psychological laboratory, partly as a consequence of the dissemination of statistical procedure for correlations and analyses of variance in the interval between the two world wars, whose proponents assumed continuous dimensions. However, most investigators in biology assumed that natural phenomena are the product of classes of entities and the specific processes in which the entities participate. The entities are usually conceptualized as patterned structures, qualitatively different from members of related classes, even though it is usually possible to invent at least one quantitative dimension on which to place members of different classes. The concept of species, of course, is a qualitative category.

I believe the two temperamental types we call inhibited and uninhibited are analogous to biological strains. Each type refers to a class of children who share a genotype, an environmental history, and a set of correlated behavioral and physiological characteristics. Support for this claim comes from a recent study in our laboratory of a third longitudinal cohort of Caucasian middle- and working-class children of both sexes who were not selected initially to be extreme on the two behavioral profiles. These children represent the typical youngsters that child psychologists study in their research. The children in this third cohort were observed initially at 14 months ($n = 100$), and again at 20 ($n = 91$), 32 ($n = 76$) and 48 months of age ($n = 77$). The indexes of behavioral inhibition at 14 and 20 months were based on behavior with an unfamiliar examiner and with unfamiliar toys in laboratory rooms. The index of inhibition at 32 months was based on behavior in a 30-minute free-play situation with two other unfamiliar children of the same sex and age with all three mothers present. The index at 4 years was based on behavior with an unfamiliar child of the same sex and age, with an unfamiliar examiner in a testing situation, and in an unfamiliar room containing unfamiliar objects.

The original variation in the continuous index of inhibited behavior at 14 months across the entire group was correlated with analogous variation at 20 and 32 months ($r = 52; r = 44$). However, the indexes of inhibition at 14 or 20 months did not predict differences in behavior at 4 years of age. Only when we restricted the analysis to those children who fell at the top and bottom 20 percent of the distribution of behavioral inhibition at both 14 and 20 months (13 children in each group) did we find significant differences in behavior between the two extreme groups at 4 years of age ($t = 2.69$, $p < .01$) (Kagan, Reznick, and Gibbons 1989). We have just completed assessment of the two extreme groups at 5½ years of age using the procedures we implemented at 7½ years with the first two cohorts. The differences between the groups in shyness and sociability remain highly significant.

This corpus of evidence implies that the constructs *inhibited* and *uninhibited* refer to qualitative categories of children. They do not refer to a behavioral continuum ranging from extreme shyness to sociability in an unselected sample of children, even though such a phenotypic continuum can be constructed. Robert Hinde has also argued for the importance of qualitative categories (Hinde and Dennis 1986). Even though the self-reports of sadness from depressive patients and a random sample of adults form a continuum, psychiatrists regard the two groups as qualitatively different. The popular practice of studying the covariation among a set of continuous dimensions in a volunteer sample of children or adults is, on occasion, analogous to a behavioral biologist correlating two continuous variables on a sample consisting of several macaque species. Behavioral biologists know better.

Psychological Correlates of Inhibited and Uninhibited Temperaments

We believe that inhibited and uninhibited children are different genetically, in part, because the two groups display peripheral psychophysiological profiles implying that the inhibited children have lower thresholds of reactivity in the limbic system, especially the amygdala and its projections to the hypothalamus, sympathetic nervous system, and corpus striatum. If this supposition were valid, inhibited children should show greater reactivity in the target organs of the sympathetic nervous system, skeletal motor system, and the hypothalamic-pituitary-adrenal axis. The data we have gathered are in support of this prediction.

The consistently inhibited subjects in both cohorts had higher and more stable heart rates than uninhibited children during the early years. Further, at every age, the inhibited children in all three cohorts were more likely to show an increase in heart rate, about ten beats per minute, across the multiple trials of a test episode as well as across the entire battery of tests. The consistent tendency of inhibited children to show cardiac acceleration to mild cognitive stress suggests greater sympathetic influence on cardiovascular functioning. Further, the inhibited children in all three cohorts showed large increases in diastolic blood pressure when they were asked to change from a sitting to a standing position. This fact implies greater sympathetic tone on the vessels in the arterial tree. A third index of sympathetic tone is pupilary dilation, which was assessed at 5½ years in the first two cohorts. The inhibited children displayed larger pupil diameters during test questions as well as during baseline periods. In addition, inhibited children displayed higher muscle tension under stress. Our main index of muscle tension came from an assessment of voice quality, which is influenced by changes in the skeletal muscles of the larynx and vocal cords. Increased tension in these muscles is accomplished by a decrease in the variability of the pitch periods of vocal utterances, which is called perturbation. The inhibited, compared with uninhibited, children showed a significantly greater decrease in vocal perturbation with single words spoken under moderate as opposed to low stress.

Finally, we assessed activity in the hypothalamic-pituitary-adrenal-axis by gathering samples of saliva in the early morning on three different days from cohorts 1 and 2 at both 5½ and 7½ years. The children with cortisol values above the median of their age group at both ages were more likely to have been classified as inhibited originally than those who were below the median on both ages. And the children in the third cohort who were extremely inhibited at both 32 and 48 months had higher cortisol values at both ages than the extremely uninhibited children.

The varied psychological reactions I have described are not highly intercorrelated, but this is a common phenomenon. Thus, we create an aggregate index of physiological activity by averaging the standard scores for eight peripheral physiological variables gathered at 5½ years on cohort 1 to create a composite index of physiological arousal. There was a substantial positive relation between this composite index and the index of behavioral inhibition at every age ($r = 0.70$ with the index at 21 months; $r = 0.64$ with the index at 7½ years).

Prediction of Inhibited and Uninhibited Temperaments from Infancy

We are currently attempting to find qualities in young infants that might predict inhibited and uninhibited behavior in the second year by evaluating the behavior of Caucasian infants seen longitudinally at 2, 4, 9, and 14 months of age. We have seen 94 at all four ages out of a total sample of 102 children. The 2- and 4-month-old infants were presented with discrepant visual and auditory events while heart rate and behavior were recorded. For example, at 4 months the episodes included a series of mobiles with different numbers of elements and tape recordings of a female voice speaking syllables varying in loudness. At 9 and 14 months we observed the children in both laboratory and free-play settings while they encountered unfamiliar events and objects. For example, in one of the episodes the mother assumed a frown while she displayed a moving toy to a child. In another, a female examiner uncovered a rotating toy and spoke a nonsense phrase in an angry tone with a frown on her face. In a third, an unfamiliar woman opened a cabinet in a large playroom revealing a metal robot. After remaining quiet for a minute, she invited the child to approach and play with the robot; failure to approach was coded as fear. There were 16 episodes at 9 months and 17 episodes at 14 months of age during which the child could display fear, where fear was defined operationally as the occurance of fretting or crying to the presentation of an unfair event or failure to approach an unfamiliar woman (who had entered a large playroom and sat near the child) or failure to approach the robot described earlier.

Two obvious behavioral differences among the 4-month-old infants were degree of motor activity to the visual and auditory stimuli, as reflected in vigorous movement of the limbs, arching of the back, protrusion of the tongue, and frequency and intensity of crying to these stimuli. There is not a high correlation, for the entire sample, between motor activity and crying, although the direction of the relation is in the expected direction. But 23 percent of the infants showed a profile of high motor activity and high irritability while 37 percent showed the complementary profile of low motor activity and minimal crying. These two profiles may represent early forms of the inhibited and uninhibited categories, respectively. The remaining 40 percent of the infants showed mixed profiles (high motor activity with low crying or low motor activity with high crying).

The children who displayed both high motor activity and high crying at 4 months of age were significantly more fearful at both 9 and 14 months than the children who showed low motor activity and low crying. The former group showed an average of 5 fears at 14 months compared with 1.8 fears for the infants who showed low motor activity and low crying ($p < .01$). Not one of the high motor–high cry infants but 14 of the 35 infants who were low motor–low cry displayed low levels of fear at both 9 and 14 months.

Recent research by biologists and neuroscientists provides an initial interpretation of this interesting result. The basal area of the amygdala has a major projection to the ventral striatum and ventral pallidum which project, in turn, to the hypothalamus. Infants with a low threshold of reactivity in the basal area should show high levels of motor activity to visual and auditory stimuli. The central nucleus of the amygdala exerts a significant influence on the central gray and the sympathetic nervous system and mediates distress vocalizations in animals. By extrapolation, it may have an important influence on crying in infants. Further, the basal area synapses on the central nucelus and, therefore, activity in the former can influence the latter. Thus, an infant with a low threshold of arousal for both the basal and central areas should show both high motor activity and crying when presented with changing or unfamiliar stimulation.

It is of interest that Dunn and Everitt (1988) at Cambridge University have written that the amygdala mediates avoidance of unfamiliar foods in rats, and they suggest that this is one of the structures mediating states of fear.

I believe that the combination of high motor activity and high irritability at 4 months of age and fearful, inhibited behavior at 9 and 14 months may be due to the presence of a lower threshold of excitability in both the basal and central areas of the amygdala. Given the total corpus of evidence presented, this is not a wild idea.

However, the bases for a lower threshold in those parts of the amygdala are multiple. A low threshold could be due to higher levels of either central norepinephrine or a corticotropin-releasing hormone—the latter is secreted by the amygdala as well as the hypothalamus—or a lower density of receptors for opioids, which would lead to modulation of excitability of the neurons in this structure. Each of these very different mechanisms could be influenced by genetic factors.

However, all newborn infants born with an amygdala that is easily aroused by unfamiliarity do not grow up to be inhibited children. I believe the eventual display of inhibited behavior in the second year of life requires some form of environmental stress in order to actualize the temperamental disposition. Relevant stressors include marital quarrels, illness in the family, or the presence of a dominating older sibling. In all three cohorts more inhibited children had older siblings while more uninhibited children were firstborn. The presence of an older brother or sister can be a stressor to some children because the older child teases and responds noncontingently to the infant. If an infant were born with the biological qualities that favor later inhibition, these daily events could function as the chronic stress needed to actualize the temperamental disposition. However, firstborn children with the same temperamental characteristics living in a minimally stressful environment would be less likely to become inhibited children.

Conclusion

Attributing some of the variation in social behavior to inherited biological processes alters the traditional post-Enlightenment view of our relation to nature. It is difficult to resist the conclusion that temperamentally inhibited 5-year-olds are potential victims of circumstances over which they have little control, rather than autonomous agents who can, at will, alter their behavior toward others. A resolution of this tension is possible if we award to each child's consciousness the power to attempt to cope with his or her temperamental bias. I recall an adult subject in the Fels longitudinal study who had been an extremely inhibited boy and became a theoretical physicist. He told me that, as an adolescent, he had been very apprehensive with girls but decided to overcome his fear by inviting the most attractive girl in the class to the senior high school dance. Human behavior is, some of the time, the product of the imposition of deliberate processes on the invisible, uncontrollable forces of biology and history. Although Homer believed Odysseus could do little to subvert Athena's decision to beach him high on a rock in the middle of a storm, Dylan Thomas exhorts us to "rage, rage against the dying of the light."

References

Bowlby, J. (1969). *Attachment*. New York: Basic Books.

Cairns, R., and Hood, K. E. (1983). Continuity in social development. In *Life span development*, Vol. 5, ed. P. Baltes and O. G. Brim, 301–358. New York: Academic Press.

Cummings, E. M., Zahn-Waxler, C., and Radke-Yarrow, M. (1981). Young children's responses to expressions of anger and affection by others in the family. *Child Development* 52:1274–82.

Diamond, A. (1983). *Behavioral changes between six and twelve months*. Ph.D. diss., Harvard University.

Dunn, L. T., and Everitt, B. J. (1988). Double dissociations of the effects of the amygdala and insular cortex lesions on conditioned taste aversion passive avoidance, and neophobia in the rat using the excitotoxin, ibotenic acid. *Behavioral Neurosciences* 102:3–9.

Ellis, H. (1900). The analysis of the sexual impulse. *The Alienist and Neurologist* 21:247–62.

Garcia-Coll, C., Kagan, J., and Reznick, J. S. (1984). Behavior inhibition in young children. Child Development 55:1005–1019.

Gersten, M. (1986). The contribution of temperament to behavior and natural context. Ed.D. diss., Graduate School of Education.

Hinde, R. A., and Dennis A. (1986). Categorizing individuals. *International Journal of Behavioral Development* 9:105–19.

Kagan, J (1981). *The second year*. Cambridge: Harvard University Press.

Kagan J. (1989). Temperamental contributions to social behavior. *American Psychologist* 44:664–68.

Kagan, J., Kearsley, R., and Zelazo, P. (1978). *Infancy: Its place in human development.* Cambridge: Harvard University Press.

Kagan, J., and Moss, H. A. (1962). *Birth to Maturity.* New York: John Wiley & Sons.

Kagan, J., Reznick, J. S., and Gibbons, J. (1989). Inhibited and uninhibited types of children. *Child Development* 60:838–45.

Kagan, J., Reznick, J. S., and Snidman, N. (1987). The physiology and psychology of behavioral inhibition in children. *Child Development* 58:1459–73.

Kagan, J., Reznick, J. S., and Snidman, N. (1988). Biological bases of childhood shyness. *Science* 240:167–71.

Mason, W. A. (1978). Social experience and primate cognitive development. In *The development of behavior: Comparative and evolutionary aspects,* ed. G. M. Burghardt and M. Bekoff, 233–51. New York: Garland Press.

Matheny, A. P. (1989). Children's behavioral inhibition over age and across situations. *Journal of Personality* 57:215–35.

Moss, H. A., and Susman, E. J. (1980). Longitudinal study of personality development. In *Constancy and Change in Human Development,* ed. O. G. Brim and J. Kagan, 530–95. Cambridge: Harvard University Press.

Olweus, D. (1981). Stability in aggressive, inhibited, and withdrawn behavior patterns. Paper presented at meeting of the Society for Research in Child Development, Boston, April.

Petitto, L. A. (1983). From gesture to symbol. Ph.D. diss., Harvard University Graduate School of Education.

Rathburn, C., DiVirgilio, L., and Waldfogel, S. (1958). A restitutive process in children following radical separation from family and culture. *American Journal of Orthopsychiatry* 28:408–15.

Reznick, J. S., Kagan, J., Snidman, N., Gersten, M., Baak, J., and Rosenberg, A. (1986). Inhibited and uninhibited behavior. *Child Development* 51:660–80.

Sheldon, W. H. (1940). *The Varieties of Human Physique,* New York: Harper.

Starkey, P., Spelke, E., and Gelman, R. (1983). "Detection of intermodal numeral correspondence by human infants." *Science* 222:175–181.

Stern, W. (1930). *Psychology of Early Childhood.* 6th ed. New York: Henry Holt.

Winick, M., Myer, K. K., and Harris, R. C. (1975). Malnutrition and environmental enrichment by early adoption. *Science* 190:1173–75.

Chapter 3

Uptight and Laid-Back Monkeys: Individual Differences in the Response to Social Challenges

Stephen J. Suomi

In this chapter I will present data collected over the last eight years focusing on individual differences in certain behavioral traits among rhesus monkeys that appear to be critical in mitigating responses to environmental novelty and challenge. These personality-like characteristics are predictively useful in determining how individual monkeys cope with changes and challenges in their social and physical environment throughout their lives. Some monkeys consistently respond to such changes and challenges with physiological and behavioral reactions that are unusually strong in terms of magnitude and duration, relative to those displayed by most rhesus monkeys faced with the same environmental circumstances.

There is compelling evidence that these behavioral and physiological differences in characteristic response to environmental novelty and challenge are highly heritable. When basic environmental circumstances are maintained in a fairly stable fashion, these differences remain remarkably stable for an individual over time, spanning major periods of development. This is particularly true for the physiological components of these different profiles of response. Yet, we have found, and are currently exploring, the degree to which these behavioral and physiological profiles show plasticity, at least under certain environmental circumstances and along certain dimensions. The results have implications not only for a general understanding of the development of personality characteristics in a nonhuman primate species but also for both theoretical and applied issues concerning individual differences in response to challenge within human populations, especially those at risk for developing various anxiety and depressive disorders.

The basic premise underlying this work is the notion that careful study of social development in rhesus monkeys can provide insights into basic developmental trends in other primate species, including humans. In developing this argument I will first describe some of the features of rhesus monkey social life. Later I will characterize some dramatic individual differences in patterns of social adjustment in this species as well as the environmental circumstances that generate or exaggerate these differences. I will also describe the physiological correlates of these behaviors, as well as how they typically change across time and situations. Finally, I will describe some of our attempts to modify particular components of these behavioral response patterns with both pharmacological and behaviorally based interventions.

The Rhesus Monkey as a Model for Social Development

Rhesus monkeys (*Macaca mulatta*) are probably the world's second most successful primate species—after humans—on virtually every population and demographic dimension. There are currently more rhesus monkeys living in the wild than any other nonhuman primate species. These resourceful primates can be found over a greater geographical area than any other nonhuman primate species, ranging over the entire subcontinent of India. Their natural habitats span such dramatically different climatic regions as humid jungles, hot and arid savannas, and even the foothills of the Himalayas in Nepal, Tibet, Pakistan, and Afghanistan, where the winters are cold and harsh. In India they not only inhabit areas that are remote from human habitation but also can be found living comfortably in the middle of India's largest cities. In the wild and in those captive environments that provide sufficient space, these animals typically live in large social groups (called *troops*) consisting of anywhere from twenty to several hundred individuals.

Macaque social groups are quite complicated and rigorous in their social structure. The basic mode of social organization consists of several multigenerational matrilines. This occurs because females normally remain in the troop in which they were born (natal troop) for their entire lifetime, whereas males emigrate from their natal troop at adolescence and often may change troops again several times during their lifetime. Rhesus monkey troops are characterized not only by matriarchal kinship lines but also by complex dominance hierarchies both among and within each of the matriarchal lineages, as well as among the adult males in the troop, who, while genetically unrelated to the adult females, are otherwise well integrated into the group. As a result, young monkeys must acquire a very complicated repertoire of social skills, as well as a substantial amount of social knowledge about individuals in the group. This requires, at the very least, sophisticated individual recognition skills as well as mnemonic and cognitive abilities enabling the monkeys to associate individuals with the lineages from which they were derived. This capability is extremely important, because kinship and dominance relationships are both complicated and unforgiving. Animals that make mistakes (for example, choose to side with somebody who doesn't get along with their matriarchal line or misread an alliance) are apt to suffer severe consequences, including serious injury or death.

Thus, young rhesus monkeys must acquire a vast amount of both social information and skills during development. They must be able to cope with periodic challenges from predators, with challenges and competition from individuals in other rhesus monkey troops, and with the dynamic changes within the dominance hierarchies of their own group. Most rhesus monkeys manage to master these challenges, and this is probably why the species occupies so many environmental niches so successfully. It also makes rhesus monkeys a fascinating species for studying socialization and developmental processes in primates.

Social connections and challenges begin from the first day of life for rhesus monkey infants. Figure 3.1 shows a 4-hour-old infant clinging to its mother in one of our outdoor environments at the National Institutes of Health Animal Center. From the beginning of life, rhesus monkey infants are surrounded by kin and maintained in tight social groups. During their first days and weeks individual infants spend almost all of their time on or in very close proximity to their biological mothers. The advantages of such proximity to the mother are ob-

Figure 3.1
Four-hour-old rhesus monkey neonate with its mother. The monkey in the foreground is the mother's sister.

vious—not only is there a ready source of nourishment (assuming the mother is in reasonably good health), but the mother also provides contact comfort, first described by Harlow (1958). Contact comfort refers to the psychological security acquired through experience with tactile contact with another individual. In higher primate species such as the macaques this contact is crucial for maintaining and directing the socialization process. In addition to providing psychological warmth, staying on or close to a mother affords the infant access to a heat source. Neonatal rhesus monkey infants, like other newborn primates, do not have full thermal regulatory capabilities during their first two weeks of life. Few heat sources can provide as many additional benefits as the infant's mother (Harlow and Suomi 1970).

Adult male rhesus monkeys have virtually nothing to do with caretaking of newborn infants and tend to have very few interactions with youngsters until they grow to late childhood or early adolescence. This may be largely due to the fact that rhesus monkey mothers are extraordinarily possessive and protective, and they typically exclude all but close female kin from contact with their infants. Consequently rhesus monkey males rarely get particularly close to infants. This pattern of exclusive maternal caregiving is a species-typical pattern that is relatively resistant to environmental modification.

Harlow (1971) designed a laboratory environment in which males, females, and their offspring were compelled to live in a monogamous family arrangement (see figure 3.2). In this environment adult male and female pairs and their offspring shared a single living unit located close to a central play area where infants were able to interact with individuals from other families. Adults could not squeeze through the openings connecting the family living space with the play area. Consequently the adults were restricted to their home cages in forced monogamy. However, even under these circumstances, the males spent less than 5 percent of their time physically interacting with infants, even though they had ample opportunity to do so (Suomi 1977a).

When adult males do interact with the infants, they are often quite incompetent. In figure 3.2 the mother is holding the infant in ventral-ventral contact. This contrasts sharply with the behavior of the male displayed in figure 3.3, in which the infant is being held upside down and placed on the adult's hip, rather than on its ventral surface. Parenthetically, it is not beyond a male rhesus monkey's power to acquire reasonable caretaking skills when no female caregivers are available (Redican 1976). Nevertheless, these capabilities are not normally expressed in natural social situations.

During the second month of life rhesus monkey infants begin to stray from their mothers for brief periods in order to explore and in-

Figure 3.2
Rhesus monkey infant with its biological mother and father. Note that the father is grooming the mother but is not touching the infant.

teract with new aspects of their physical and social environment. They do this in a characteristic manner, using their mother as a secure base in much the same way as do human infants and toddlers (Bowlby 1969). Gradually, in succeeding weeks and months these exploratory forays become more frequent and involve larger distances away from the mother. Nevertheless, the mother remains the pivot from which the infant explores the world. Indeed the importance of the mother continues to be crucial at this "toddler stage," even though the amount of physical contact maintained with the mother decreases markedly.

It can be shown experimentally that removal of the mother reduces all types of infant exploratory behavior dramatically and causes the infant to become quite upset (Seay, Hansen, and Harlow 1962). This remains true despite the fact that during the second and third month of life rhesus infants acquire substantial locomotor skills that enable them to spend an increasing amount of time physically away from their mothers (cf. Harlow and Harlow 1965). As a result the infants begin to come into frequent contact with other members of their social group beyond their kin, including peers born during the same birth season in their social group. In the wild this is not coincidental; rhesus monkeys, although sexually active year-round, have a circum-

Figure 3.3
Inept handling of infant monkey by its biological father.

scribed period of breeding and consequently a circumscribed birth season. As many as 80 percent of the infants in a group are typically born during a two- or three-month period rather than spread out over the entire year. For this reason every individual born within this period is likely to have many peers with approximately the same degree of physical and social competence with whom to interact.

Initially, early peer interactions among rhesus monkey infants are scarcely different from the infants' manipulations of inanimate objects. Infants typically pull and pick and bite away on anything they find, regardless of whether it is a branch or another monkey. They quickly learn, however, that although inanimate objects cannot initiate or reciprocate activity, their peers can and do. Thus, by 3 or 4 months of age, new types of social relationships emerge involving age-mate friendships that are fundamentally different from their relationships with their mothers (Harlow 1969; Suomi and Harlow 1975).

Age-mate friendships are characterized by relatively loose bonds among many individuals. This is in contrast to the strong, unique bond between infant and mother. The behaviors encompassing or fostering age-mate friendships are very different from those involved in mother-infant interactions. In time, especially after 6 months of age, interactions with peers come to predominate and make up most of the young monkey's daytime activity.

Figure 3.4 shows data from a study conducted at the University of Wisconsin (Suomi 1977b) within a typically complex social environment. The figure shows the target of the infant's socialization during its first 50 months of life, presenting a quantitative profile for (a) infants' initiation to mothers; (b) infants' initiation to other infants in the group of peers; and (c) infants' initiation to other adults in the group. As can be seen, interactions with the mother drop off substantially during the first 6 months of life and remain fairly low thereafter. Rhesus monkey infants rarely interact with other adults even when such opportunities exist. On the other hand, interactions with peers increase dramatically around 6 months of age, and they remain high throughout the first year of life and, in fact, into early adolescence. For rhesus monkeys adolescence typically begins in the fourth year of life for males and the end of the third year for females, when each becomes physically capable of reproduction. At this time peer interactions begin to decline for both males and females.

The nature of play behavior changes markedly during the juvenile period. At 4 months play behaviors consist mainly of short bouts of activity of only a few seconds' duration. The play behavior almost always involves a simple sequence of activities with a single partner (an initiation followed by a response, perhaps followed by a recipro-

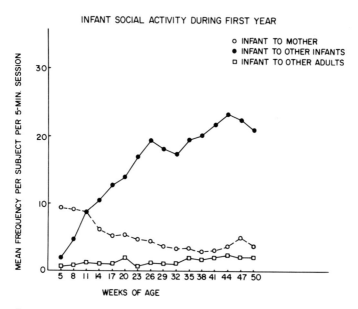

Figure 3.4
Relative frequencies of behavior directed by young monkeys during their first 50 months of life toward (a) their mother, (b) other infants, and (c) other adults (from Suomi 1977b).

cation of that response). One individual may chase another, as shown in figure 3.5. Then the roles reverse and the chaser becomes the one who is chased.

Figure 3.6 shows 2- and 3-year-old rhesus monkeys playing. The total daily amount of time spent playing is nearly the same as for their younger counterparts, but the play activities are much more complicated. These activities usually involve more than two individuals and typically last from several minutes to as long as 30 minutes or more. The sequence of play activities at this age are extraordinarily complex. Quite frequently coalitions form and then reverse themselves. Furthermore, embedded in the sequences are what appear to be precursors, or elementary forms, of adaptive behaviors that, in adulthood, are used to coordinate reproductive and social activities.

It is now well established (Harlow and Harlow 1965; Suomi and Harlow 1978) that rhesus monkeys deprived of the opportunities to develop these behaviors through peer play are almost always hyper-aggressive and often unsuccessful in reproductive activities later in adulthood. For the most part, play patterns are normally learned in same-sex subgroups. By the time they are 4 to 5 months old, rhesus

Figure 3.5
Play bout between 4-month-old rhesus monkey peers.

Figure 3.6
Rough-and-tumble play bout between 2- and 3-year-old monkeys.

monkey juveniles begin to segregate themselves by sex in their play bouts. The sex segregation is expanded and exaggerated through the second year of life but begins to change at puberty. The causes for this seem similar to those described for human children (Maccoby 1980). Typically males engage in more rough-and-tumble play initiations, and by 6 months of age most females stop reciprocating. Moreover, females seldom initiate rough-and-tumble activities themselves; instead they spend more time in grooming and chasing bouts with other females. In general males are less choosy in selecting play partners and seem willing to play with anyone who reciprocates. Interestingly, these gender differences are enhanced when adults are present (cf. Suomi and Harlow 1978). Thus there is apparently a social as well as a biological component to gender-specific play activities.

Although social play dominates the waking hours of rhesus monkeys throughout childhood, play and even interactions with peers begin to decrease as these animals approach adolescence. At puberty males and females go their separate ways, particularly in the wild. Males are literally ejected from their home group at puberty if they do not leave voluntarily. In both semiwild and feral environments, nonfamilial adult females typically force adolescent males to emigrate. Curiously, the pubertal males' relatives provide virtually no support, and the adult males in the troop do not intervene. Consequently adolescent males have little choice but to leave their natal groups. Most of these males subsequently join all-male gangs for a few months before they finally work their way into a new troop.

There is some evidence that age-mate friendships developed earlier during childhood can persist in these all-male gangs and may even play a role after the males work their way into new troops. Entering a new group is almost certainly the most complex and daunting challenge facing a young male rhesus monkey. In most cases the existing members of the new group have no interest in accepting these young adult males. Thus males must bring to bear all of their social skills in order to integrate themselves successfully into a new troop.

Although earlier studies generally reported that males never reenter their natal troops, there is now some evidence (cf. Rasmussen and Fellowes in preparation) that they certainly try. New evidence also indicates that young adult males hang around the edges of their natal troops before joining the all-male gangs and eventually attempting to enter a new troop. Under some circumstances males may enter new troops by following older brothers into existing troops. A different strategy that has also been observed is for young males to move into the middle of a new troop and take on all challengers. Although risky, such a strategy can work if the new troop has few adult males at the time and may provide a "fast track" for a young male to become a dominant member of the group. An alternative strategy is for the young male to hang out on the periphery of a new troop, make friends with low-ranking animals, and then gradually work into the center of the troop. This strategy takes more time but is probably considerably less dangerous.

Young adulthood is clearly a very difficult time for both male and female rhesus monkeys. Some studies report that as many as 40 to 50 percent of males in this age group die within a year of leaving their natal troops (cf. Dittus 1979). Females, in contrast, usually remain in their natal groups throughout life, in close association with their mother and other maternal kin. This results in the establishment and maintenance of long-term multigenerational matriarchal kinship lines. There seems to be substantial long-term benefits for the young females, not only in staying physically close to the mother but also in sharing her status in the dominance hierarchy of the social group. One consequence of this phenomenon is that when young females have their own infants (particularly their first), they are usually provided with substantial social support from kin. This highlights the adaptive significance of multigenerational matrilines for this species. For young adult females in the wild, the dangers associated with first pregnancy and successful parturition are almost always mitigated by social support from close kin, usually the mother. Adult females not only provide help in infant care but also serve to ward off predators and competitors in the process.

This, then, is basically the sequence of life events and developmental milestones characterizing rhesus monkey social-behavioral ontogeny from birth to maturity. The sequence follows a predictable course in virtually all individuals. Strong attachments to the mother are gradually loosened as multiple peer friendships are developed. At puberty, males and females go their separate ways. Despite these similar patterns, there are striking individual differences in how rapidly and easily particular monkeys move from one developmental stage to another. This is the subject of the next portion of this chapter.

Developmental Differences in Coping with Social Changes and Challenges

The data I will present are derived from studies of individual behavior in a self-sufficient breeding colony of rhesus monkeys. In this group we have identified some individuals, about 20 percent of the population, who respond to changes in their physical and social environment with extreme behavioral and physiological disruption. These animals appear to be unusually fearful or anxious and very shy. They withdraw in the presence of stimuli that other monkeys in their group readily approach. In everyday conversation we have used the term *uptight* to describe the behavioral characteristics of these individuals when faced with challenge or change. In contrast, other monkeys with exactly the same backgrounds, faced with exactly the same situations, seem much more relaxed. They respond to change or challenge less intensely and adjust quickly to new situations. These animals are much more *laid back* than their uptight counterparts. Although dramatic changes in their environment may produce transient behavioral and physiological disruption for these individuals, the effects are more brief and less dramatic than for the uptight counterparts. About 80 percent of our population can be described as being largely laid back.

We have found that these differences in response to novelty and challenge show up very early in life and are quite stable over the life span. They first become evident at the time that infants begin to stray from their mother to explore the environment. Some infants stray farther away for longer periods of time. Later, when these monkeys begin to interact with peers, we find that those who were the first to stray from their mothers are usually the first to initiate interactions with peers. They are also the first to take advantage of new toys and other amenities in their play area. Conversely, those individuals who were most reluctant to leave their mother are more withdrawn in early social interactions with age-mates.

In a recent study, 4-month-old monkeys were placed in a social playroom for the first time and paired with unfamiliar partners for one-hour sessions. Half of the monkeys had previously been judged to be high-reactive (uptight) behaviorally while the other half were judged to be more relaxed (laid back). This paradigm is very similar to that described by Kagan, Reznick, and Snideman (1987) in a study of inhibited and uninhibited human children. In Kagan et al.'s paradigm, human children were scored by observers judging behavioral inhibition while they interacted for the first time in a playroom filled with a variety of toys and objects that promote physical activity. Predictably, some individuals—both human and monkey—took full advantage of the play opportunities in this setting, while others were much more withdrawn.

Physiological measures for the two groups of young monkeys (uptight and laid back) provided more evidence of the dramatic difference between these two groups. Heart rate levels for the first and last five minutes of the one-hour sessions are shown in figure 3.7. The behaviorally reactive animals initially showed somewhat higher heart rates and less beat-to-beat variability. Over the course of the hour, the less reactive animals showed a decrease in heart rate with more

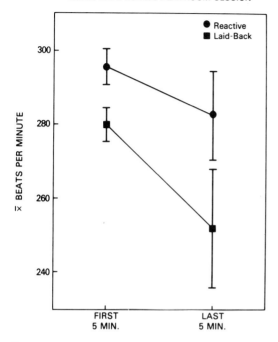

Figure 3.7
Mean (+/− SE) heart rate levels for reactive (uptight) and nonreactive (laid-back) 4-month-old rhesus monkeys during the first 5 minutes and last 5 minutes of a 1-hour session in a novel playroom. Data are based on 12 pairs of monkeys, with one member of each pair representing each reactive type.

variability, while the more behaviorally reactive individuals showed little change. In addition, we found that uptight individuals had substantially higher levels of both plasma cortisol and ACTH in this situation than laid-back monkeys. Thus, physiological correlates existed for these behavioral attributes.

When these uptight monkeys stayed in the playroom for several hours, or were reintroduced many times, both their cardiac and endocrine functions returned to normal levels, and behaviorally the distinction between reactive individuals and others diminished. But on first exposure to novelty, these differences were indeed dramatic.

Such differences in response to novelty and challenge remain quite stable as rhesus monkeys grow older. When they are placed in other settings, some individuals predictably are the first to explore the new environment, while their uptight counterparts remain in the background and scrutinize the situation carefully before beginning physical exploration. We have observed these differences in a variety of environments, including some of the outdoor settings that we initiated at the University of Wisconsin and now maintain at the NIH Animal Center. Regardless of the structure of the play situation, outcomes for specific individuals have tended to be highly predictable and stable over time.

Of interest is not only the consistency of these findings but also the fact that these differences can be identified very early in life using a variety of measures. In addition, a growing body of circumstantial evidence suggests that these differences in response to environmental novelty and challenge are highly heritable.

Evidence that this is the case is provided in figure 3.8, summarizing data from an early heart-rate conditioning study by Baysinger et al. (1978) in which nursery-reared one-month-old rhesus monkey infants were conditioned to respond to a ten-second 70 db tone immediately preceding a burst of white noise. As has been found with human children (Graham and Clifton, 1965), there is usually a decrease in heart rate during the period of orientation in anticipation of the onset

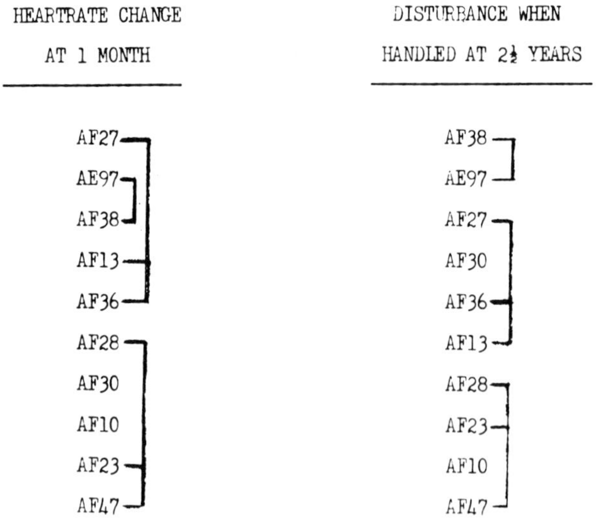

HEARTRATE CHANGE   DISTURBANCE WHEN
    AT 1 MONTH   HANDLED AT 2½ YEARS

        AF27   AF38
        AE97   AE97
        AF38   AF27
        AF13   AF30
        AF36   AF36
        AF28   AF13
        AF30   AF28
        AF10   AF23
        AF23   AF10
        AF47   AF47

Figure 3.8
Rank ordering of monkeys in terms of (a) the magnitude of heart rate change in a conditioning paradigm at 1 month of age (left column), and (b) duration of disturbance following handling for intubation at 2½ years of age (right column). Monkey identification numbers are listed in order of largest heart rate change to smallest (left column) and most disturbance to least disturbance (right column). Brackets connect paternal half siblings (subjects with the same biological father).

of the burst of white noise. Baysinger et al. (1978) found that there were considerable individual differences in the magnitude of this anticipatory response during conditioning period. Figure 3.8 shows the rank ordering of heart-rate change among the ten infant subjects tested in the study.

Two and a half years later these same monkeys were used in a different study in which saline was administered (as a control procedure) via esophageal tubes. In addition to other measurements, it was determined how quickly the animals settled down when they were placed back in their home cages following the daily tubing procedure. Significantly, virtually the same rank ordering of severity of response to handling was found for these monkeys at age 2½ as had been obtained earlier for their cardiac response.

The brackets in figure 3.8 indicate individuals who were paternal half siblings, that is, those with the same biological fathers (but different biological mothers). Since the infants were all nursery reared, the actual "mothering" experience each received was the same. Two things are evident when the data are presented in this way. First, individual monkeys tended to display the same relative ranking on both measures at both ages (i.e., these measures showed high concordance). Second, individuals tended to share the same ranking as close relatives. Using these data and others obtained in different studies (cf. Scanlan 1988), it has been possible to calculate heritability coefficients for these traits. On a variety of behavioral and physiological measures, we have found significant familial correspondence, even among individuals who have been foster reared by nonbiological parents. We have found this to be true for both paternal half siblings and maternal half siblings, and the relationship is even stronger among full siblings.

Individual Differences in Biobehavioral Responses to Brief Social Separation

It is important to note that under familiar, nonchallenging circumstances, there are few, if any, differences in behavior or in physiological reactions in the two sets of monkeys described above. The differences appear only when the monkeys are challenged (if they are briefly separated from peers or mothers or placed in a new free-play situation). If the challenge is prolonged, the differences between the uptight and laid-back monkeys become even more apparent.

For example, monkeys briefly separated from either parents or peers virtually always show an initial period of protest similar to that described for human children (Bowlby 1969). After a few hours, however, most young monkeys adjust to the separation and begin exploring their environment and attempting to reestablish other social relationships. Moreover, most animals return fairly quickly to normal sleeping and eating patterns. In contrast, the uptight monkeys become much more withdrawn or depressed (Suomi in press).

There are also major physiological differences between the uptight monkeys and their laid-back counterparts in response to brief social separation. The behaviorally reactive monkeys show much greater hypothalamic-pituitary-adrenal activity, as assessed by plasma cortisol and ACTH levels. Measures of catecholamine turnover in the central nervous system reveal lower levels of norepinepherine and higher levels of the norepinephrine metabolite MHPG (3-methoxy-4-hydroxy phenylglycol) in cerebrospinal fluid after a few days of separation. Both cardiac and sleeping patterns remain altered as well. These behavioral and physiological patterns can be reversed by treatment with antidepressant compounds, which will be discussed later in this chapter.

In many ways these uptight monkeys provide a very compelling model for human reactive depression. As is the case for many human depressives, these monkeys appear unusually fearful or anxious in novel and mildly challenging situations. When these same individuals are confronted with a more prolonged stress or challenge, they tend to show depressive reactions. Their less anxious or more laid-back counterparts, on the other hand, show rapid adjustment to these separation situations. These results are highly predictable and stable across major portions of the life span.

Figure 3.9 presents a correlation matrix for 16 individuals based on measures of the relative incidence of depressive-like huddling behavior during two series of four-day separations from peers in the first and second years of life. The animals were put back together in social

CORRELATIONS OF THE POOLED HUDDLE DEVELOPMENTAL
TREND DATA ACROSS YEARS

		YEAR TWO	
		ACUTE	CHRONIC
YEAR ONE	ACUTE	.723	.442
	CHRONIC	-.091	.989

Figure 3.9
Correlation matrix for huddling behavior during 4-day separations experienced by young rhesus monkeys at 6 months and again at 18 months of age. "Acute" and "chronic" refer to the first day and the last two days, respectively, of the separations at 6 and 18 months (from Higley 1985).

groups after the first separation series during their first year of life, then separated for another series of four-day periods during their second year of life. The labels "acute" and "chronic" in the figure refer to the first day and last two days of each separation period. Note the remarkable correspondence between both values obtained for both periods during both separations, supporting the notion that these response characteristics are highly stable over time for any given individual.

In several studies rhesus monkeys in our laboratory have been monitored from infancy through adolescence in terms of their biobehavioral responses to brief social separation. Although there are no obvious differences between the highly reactive, uptight animals and other members of the group under familiar and stable conditions, striking differences become apparent at adolescence when they are separated. Those individuals who showed extreme reactions to separation early in life also have shown extreme behavioral and physiological separation reactions in adolescence. Interestingly, the behavioral reactions they have shown as adolescents are quite different from those exhibited in childhood. More specifically, while the response of highly reactive monkeys to separation in the first two years of life is characterized by withdrawal and inactivity, during adolescence the same individuals become agitated and hyperactive following short-term separation and exhibit a great deal of repetitive stereotypic activity such as pacing or fiddling in front of their cages.

Figure 3.10 shows a graph indicating the emergence of stereotypy during social separation as a function of age. Monkeys in the first year of life almost never show this behavioral pattern in response to separation. Yet the same individuals frequently show such reactions by 3 years of age. Put another way, there is a developmental shift in the type of behavior expressed in the prototypic extreme response to separation. Despite these differences in the form of expression, there is consistency in the extreme reactions to separation shown by individuals at different points in life. In contrast, the physiological measures (cardiac conditioning responses, cortisol and ACTH levels, catecholamine turnover) do not change much over the life span. The same patterns of physiological arousal occurring early in life to challenges are generally manifested later on.

Figure 3.11 presents data from a cross-sectional study (Scanlan 1984) measuring changes in plasma cortisol levels for animals separated from their stable social group at less than 2 years of age, at 6 to 9, at 13 through 16, and at 16 to 18 years of age (relatively late in the life span of rhesus monkeys). At each age there was a very large increase in plasma cortisol levels following brief (two-hour) separation. Furthermore, individuals showing the most marked cortisol elevations at each

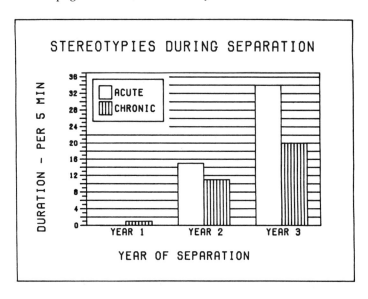

Figure 3.10
Emergence of stereotypy in response to separation as a function of increasing age.
Longitudinal data reveal dramatic increases following separation as the monkeys grow
older (from Higley 1985).

age also displayed the most extreme behavioral responses to the short-
term separation (Scanlan 1984).

Figure 3.12 illustrates a parallel set of effects in 6-month-old peer-
reared rhesus monkeys for CSF levels of catecholamine and indoleamine metabolites following four days of separation. Data are also
presented for 6-month-old maternally reared monkeys separated from
their mother and for 4-year-old adolescents separated from each other.
Data were also obtained for the mothers (aged 5 to 15 years) after
being separated from their infants. As shown in figure 3.12, these
data show that despite vast differences in age and prior experience,
virtually all subjects showed a decline in the level of norepinephrine
and an increase in the level of the norepinephrine metabolite MHPG.
There were no changes in serotonin or its metabolite 5-HIAA (5-hy-
droxyindoleacetic acid) except for the adolescent monkeys. Separation-induced increases in 5-HIAA levels appear to be a unique response,
whose basis is unclear, during this stage of development. The salient
point, however, is that for rhesus monkeys of quite different ages and
rearing backgrounds predictable neurotransmitter responses to separation can be obtained, and the magnitude of these responses appears
to parallel the magnitude of the behavioral responses.

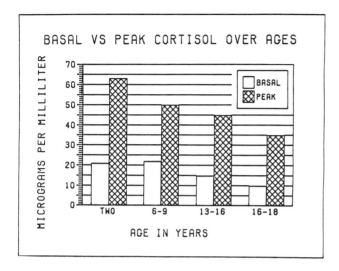

Figure 3.11
Levels of plasma cortisol from rhesus monkeys of different ages during baseline periods immediately prior to social separation (basal) and two hours following separation (peak) (from Scanlan 1984).

Figure 3.13 presents data from a study of neurotransmitter turnover in adolescent rhesus monkeys treated with the antidepressant drug imipramine hydrocloride. Responses were obtained under three different conditions: (1) when the monkeys were in their home social group receiving the drug under familiar nonchallenging circumstances; (2) when the monkeys were separated but given placebo treatments; and (3) when the monkeys were separated and given daily treatments with imipramine. The results revealed that compared to a placebo, imipramine treatment for monkeys living in normal social groups resulted in a profound decline in CSF MHPG levels (and a corresponding increase in levels of norepinephrine). There was no change in levels of the serotonin metabolite 5-HIAA, nor in levels of the dopamine metabolite HVA (homovanillic acid). Thus, under normal conditions (no particular stresses or challenges) imipramine reduces catecholamine turnover in the central nervous system. This is not surprising given the mechanism of action of the drug (it prolongs the synaptic action of catecholamines) and shows that the physiological effects of imipramine in these monkeys is consistent with the known pharmacological properties of the drug.

When the adolescent monkeys were separated and *not* given imipramine, there was a large increase in MHPG levels (and concomitant

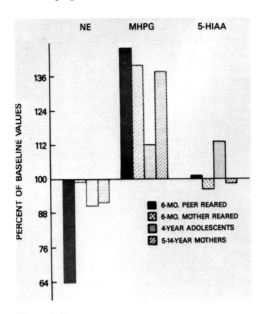

Figure 3.12
Levels of CSF norepinepherine (NE), MHPG, and 5-HIAA following four days of separation in four groups of monkeys.

decreases in CSF norephenephrine levels). There was no change in the levels of HVA and a slight (but statistically significant) increase in 5-HIAA levels.

When the monkeys were separated and given imipramine *during* the separation, the expected separation-induced increase in CSF MHPG levels (and concomitant decrease in norepinephrine) was substantially attenuated. Moreover, this effect was especially pronounced in the monkeys whose initial response to separation was most extreme. These findings suggest that response to imipramine covaries with behavioral reactivity, and they provide additional evidence linking the behavioral reactivity described here specifically to the activity of noradregenic neural networks.

Research on Cross-Fostering

Having demonstrated that anxiety and fear reactions have strong physiological and presumably genetic underpinnings, we have been especially interested in whether these characteristic behavior patterns of response to novelty and challenge (and their physiological correlates) can be modified by experience. To find out, we have adopted

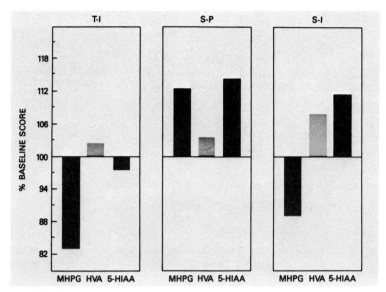

Figure 3.13
Relative changes from preseparation baseline levels of CSF MHPG, HVA, and 5-HIAA
(a) following treatment with imipramine in a group setting (T-I, left panel), (b) following placebo treatment during separation (S-P, center panel), and (c) following treatment with imipramine during separation (S-I, right panel).

the human neonatal exams of Brazelton (1973) for use with rhesus
monkey infants in order to identify highly reactive subjects as devel-
opmentally early as possible so that we can then place them with
foster mothers differing in maternal style and behavioral reactivity.

Figure 3.14 illustrates the application of one such test assessing vi-
sual- and auditory-orienting responses. In this test infants track a small
toy moved in front of them. In another test changes in muscle tone
are assessed when the infant monkey is moved in a slow sweeping
motion. We have found that these tests can be used to predict behavioral reactivity later in life. The results show that infants whose parents and close relatives are highly reactive generally show poor
orienting, slightly lower muscle tonus, and slightly poorer reflex development than controls. There are no obvious differences in temperament for these very young animals, but there is a large difference in
behavioral inhibition, as assessed by the amount of time it takes the
infant to settle down as each new test in the battery is begun (Schneider 1987). In addition to these specific tests, we also assess predominant state. Predominant state can vary from deep sleep to an active
and aroused state. Infants who show lower predominant states at the

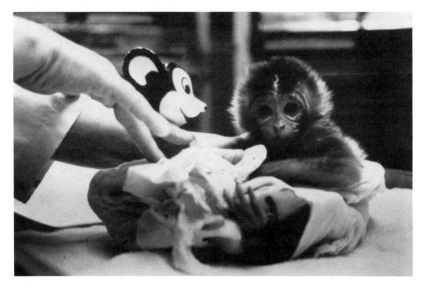

Figure 3.14
Rhesus monkey infant during visual orientating portion of neonatal test battery.

start of each examination (they appear less alert, more likely to to be in agitated sleep, and less attentive) tend to have relatives who are highly reactive (Scanlan 1988).

Individual differences in the result of infant behavioral testing appear during the first 30 days of life and are highly correlated with the behavioral characteristics of adult family members (Suomi 1987). Thus, individuals seem to inherit this tendency toward emotional and behavioral reactivity. We have been able to identify members of our breeding colony who have consistently produced offspring who are highly reactive. Other members of the breeding colony have consistently produced infants who are low reactors.

We have recently completed a study in which rhesus monkey infants that have been identified as either high or low reactive by infant testing have been cross-fostered by unrelated females who also differ in maternal style in order to better characterize the social and environmental factors controlling the development of these behavioral traits. In this study (Suomi 1987) maternal style was varied along two dimensions. The first dimension was nurturance. Some rhesus monkey mothers are very nurturant, in that they are unusually protective and supportive of their infants, and in general they are less punitive and rejecting of their offspring at weaning than are other rhesus monkey mothers. The second dimension of maternal style investigated in this study was the foster mothers' own characteristic response to challenge, as determined from previous observations of how these adult females had responded during brief periods of separation. The design of the study consisted of placing, within the first week of life, infants known to be at high or low risk for high reactivity (based on their pedigree and on their neonatal test scores) with mothers whose nurturing style and reactivity characteristics were also known.

Figure 3.15 shows data from the infants' neonatal tests as a function of their own reactivity, their foster mothers' reactivity, and their foster mothers' maternal style. With the exception of muscle tonus, there was virtually no covariance between either foster mother nurturing style and foster mother behavioral reactivity and the composite behavioral scores obtained for the infants. Clearly, for these infants the only significant predictor of scores on the neonatal measures was the infants' pedigree.

There were no obvious differences between the high- and low-reactive infants in the presence of their foster mothers during their first 6 months of life on a variety of behavioral measures including ventral contact, locomotion, exploration, and self-directed behavior. All of these cross-fostered infants showed species-normative developmental declines in mother-infant contact and increases in locomotor and exploratory behavior during their first 6 months of life (figure 3.16).

A somewhat different picture emerged when comparing the behavior of the infants placed with nurturant foster mothers with those placed with more punitive mothers. Regardless of the infants' relative reactivity, they tended to reduce ventral contact with their foster mothers earlier if these females were highly punitive. The infants also tended to show slightly more exploration and more self-directed disturbance behavior, especially around the time of weaning, if their foster mothers were more punitive.

At 6 months of age, these infants were separated from their foster mothers for four brief periods. Interestingly, during the period of separation, we found the infants' behavior strongly correlated with their pedigree. Infants from highly reactive biological parents, when separated from their foster mothers at 6 months of age, showed significantly more self-directed disturbance behavior than those with low reactive pedigrees. Such high reactive monkeys also exhibited less coping behavior, as indexed by levels of locomotion and exploration, they were generally more passive, and they had higher levels of plasma cortisol and greater CNS norepinephrine turnover (cf. Suomi 1987). Thus despite apparently good adjustment most of the time in the presence of their mothers, the behavior of these animals reflected that of their biological relatives when challenged by short-term separations.

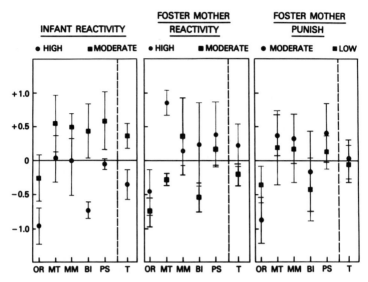

Figure 3.15
Mean (+/− 1 S.E.M.) Z-score values for five components of rhesus monkey neonatal
test battery (Schneider, 1984), plus total composite score. Values are averaged over the
four weekly test sessions during the infants' first month of life. Panel on left plots
infant scores grouped by infant reactivity pedigree (high-reactive vs. moderately reactive). Center panel plots infant scores grouped by foster mother reactivity (high vs.
moderate). Panel on right plots infant scores grouped by foster mother caretaking style
(moderately punitive vs. low-punitive). Ordinate is scaled in Z-score values derived
from the population of both mother-reared and nursery-reared infants born in the laboratory colony during 1982–1984. Abbreviations (on abscissa) for components of neonatal test battery are as follows: OR = orienting responses, MT = muscle tonus, MM
= motor maturity, BI = behavioral inhibition (high scores designate low behavioral
inhibition), PS predominant Prechtl state, T = total composite score (from Suomi 1987).

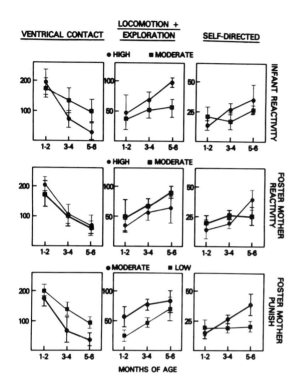

Figure 3.16
Mean duration in seconds (+/− S.E.M.) of infant behaviors during cross-fostering period. Top panels plot values grouped by infant reactivity pedigree, center panels plot values grouped by foster mother reactivity, and low panels plot values grouped by foster mother maternal style (from Suomi 1987).

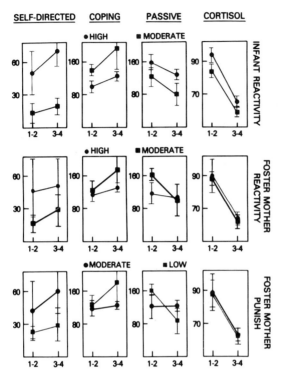

Figure 3.17
Mean values (+/− S.E.M.) of infants' scores during separation periods. Scores are durations (in seconds) per 5-minute observation period for self-directed coping, and passive categories of behavior, and micrograms per deciliter for plasma cortisol collected 2 hours after the start of each separation. Top panels plot values grouped by infant reactivity pedigree, center panel plots values grouped by foster mother reactivity, and lower panels plot values grouped by foster mother maternal style (from Suomi 1987).

Figure 3.17 shows that differences in pedigree accounted for much more of the variance in the infants' responses to separation than did differences in their foster mothers' reactivity or nurturing style. These characteristics of the foster mothers were essentially irrelevant for predicting how the infants and juveniles responded when separated. Interestingly, when these infants were returned to their foster mothers after each separation, the individual differences in infant reactivity again appeared to be inconsequential (see figure 3.18). Typically, all the individuals showed very large increases in ventral contact, followed by decreased exploration and, typically, some behavioral disturbance.

In interpreting these results, it must be noted that the foster mothers also displayed differences in the way they reacted to these brief separations. In fact, the best predictor of individual differences in the postreunion behavior of the infants was the reaction of the foster mothers to the separation. Infants with highly reactive mothers showed more contact initially and maintained a high level of contact for a longer period of time than those with low-reactive mothers. Such infants also exhibited less exploration and higher levels of disturbance during the reunion period. These findings suggest that the reunion behaviors of these infants were at least in part a response to the activity of their foster mothers, who became increasingly disturbed with each separation. Summarizing the results of this study, the best predictor of the infants' behavior in the absence of a stressor was how their foster mothers treated them. In the presence of a stressor (separation) the best predictor of the infants' behavior was family pedigree. In the presence of a stressor and in the company of an object of social support (reunion) the best predictor of individual infant behavior was the competence of the source of social support.

In a follow-up study the same cross-fostered subjects were permanently separated from their foster mothers at 8 or 9 months of age and assembled into peer groups. We found, predictably, that the highly reactive monkeys had more trouble adjusting to the novel peer groups and settling down than did the others. We then introduced an old male-female pair (colloquially called "foster grandparents") to each peer group. This was done to facilitate the socialization of peer group members—the old male effectively broke up fights and controlled the more rambunctious males in the peer group, while the old female was available for those infants in the social group desiring ventral contact.

The results were surprising (cf. Suomi 1987). Under these circumstances, individuals with a highly reactive pedigree who had been raised by a nurturing foster mother immediately established social relationships with these older individuals, particularly with the old

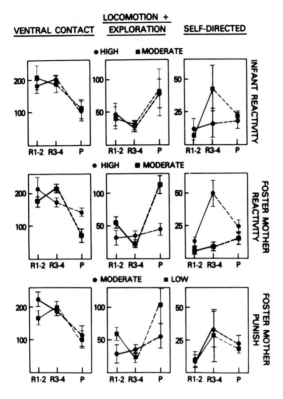

Figure 3.18
Mean durations (in seconds) per 5-minute observation period (+/− S.E.M.) for infant behaviors during reunion periods and over the 1-month period immediately following final separation and reunion. R1-2 = mean durations during first and second reunions, R3-4 = mean durations during third and fourth reunions, and Post = mean durations during 1-month post-separation period. Top panels plot values grouped by infant reactivity pedigree, middle panels plot values grouped by foster mother reactivity, and lower panels plot values grouped by foster mother maternal style.

female. Furthermore, with the old adults providing a basis of social support, these highly reactive subjects became the most dominant members of their peer groups. In contrast, those individuals who had a highly reactive pedigree, but who had been reared by punitive foster mothers, avoided the older monkeys and wound up at the bottom of the dominance hierarchy. Individuals who were less reactive, independent of the kind of foster mothers with whom they had been reared, also did not establish relationships with the older animals, and they achieved intermediate positions within the dominance hierarchy of their social group. In other words, in this particular social arrangement reactive individuals who would otherwise be at high risk for poor adjustment (including depressive reactions), and who would be most likely to wind up at the bottom of the dominance hierarchy, came to have dominant status in the group.

The above observations have led us to pursue new experimental paradigms for studying the effects of nurturance and mothering styles on behavioral development by extending the cross-fostering studies to more complex outdoor environments. Using these paradigms, we can take highly reactive infants, cross-foster them with particularly protective females, and then follow their development in much more varied environments than would be possible within the confines of an indoor laboratory. In addition, we can study the effect of rearing individuals in situations where they have substantial support from peers and older experienced individuals. Of particular interest is how these early experiences affect the ability of highly reactive males to work their way into a new troop. We can also study the efficacy of pharmacological interventions involving antidepressant and anxiolytic compounds in conjunction with behavioral manipulations to assess the extent to which these differences in reactivity can be altered or modified. Using these techniques, we believe we can continue to shed light on critically important, genetically based, yet environmentally malleable patterns of behavioral characteristics—those that enable individuals to mitigate stress and anxiety in response to social and environmental challenges.

References

Baysinger, C. M., Suomi, S. J., Cronin, C., and Ohman, L. E. (1987). Infant rhesus monkey heartrate predicts behavioral levels later in life. *Abstracts of the American Society of Primatology* 1:2–3.

Bowlby, J. (1969). *Attachment and loss: Attachment.* New York: Basic Books.

Brazelton, T. B. (1973). *Neonatal behavioral assessment scale.* London: Spastics International Medical Publications.

Dittus, W. P. J. (1979). The evolution of behaviours regulating density and age specific sex ratios in a primate population. *Behaviour* 69:265–302.

Graham, F., and Clifton, R. (1966). Heartrate change as a component of orienting reflex. *Psychological Bulletin* 65:305–20.

Harlow, H. F. (1985). The nature of love. *American Psychologist* 13:673–85.

Harlow, H. F. (1969). Age-mate or peer affectional system. In *Advances in the study of behavior*, Vol. 2, ed. D. Lehrman, R. Hinde, and E. Shaw. New York: Academic Press.

Harlow, H. F., and Harlow, M. K. (1965). The affectional systems. In *Behavior of nonhuman primates*, Vol. 2, ed. A. Schrier, H. Harlow, and F. Stollnitz. New York: Academic Press.

Harlow, H. F., and Suomi, S. J. (1970) The nature of love—simplified. *American Psychologist* 25:161–68.

Harlow, M. K. (1971). Nuclear family apparatus. *Behavior Research Methods and Instrumentation* 3:301–4.

Higley J. D. (1985). Continuity of social separation behaviors in rhesus monkeys from infancy to adolescence. Ph.D. diss., University of Wisconsin-Madison.

Kagan, J., Reznick, J. S., and Snideman, N. (1987). The physiology and psychology of behavioral inhibition in children. *Child Development* 58:1459–73.

Maccoby, E. E. (1980). *Social development: Psychological growth and the parent-child relationship*. New York: Harcourt Brace Jovanovich.

Rasmussen, K. L. R., and Fellowes, J. (In preparation).

Redican, W. K. (1976). Adult male-infant interactions in nonhuman primates. In *The role of the father in child development*, ed. M. Lamb. New York: John Wiley & Sons.

Scanlan, J. M. (1984). Adrenocortical and behavioral responses to acute novel and stressful conditions: The influence of gonadal status, timecourse of response, age, and motor activity. Master's thesis, University of Wisconsin at Madison.

Scanlan, J. M. (1988). Continuity of stress responsivity in infant rhesus monkeys (*Macaca mulatta*): State, hormonal, dominance, and genetic influences. Ph.D. diss., University of Wisconsin-Madison.

Schneider, M. L. (1987). A rhesus monkey model of human infant individual differences. Ph.D. diss., University of Wisconsin-Madison.

Seay, B. M., Hansen, E. W., and Harlow, H. F. (1962). Mother-infant separation in monkeys. *Journal of Child Psychology and Psychiatry* 3:123–32.

Suomi, S. J. (1977a). Adult male interactions among monkeys living in nuclear families. *Child Development* 48:1255–70.

Suomi, S. J. (1977b). The development of attachment and other social behaviors in rhesus monkeys. In *Attachment behavior*, ed. L. Krames, T. Alloway, and P. Pliner. New York: Plenum Press.

Suomi, S. J. (1987). Genetic and environmental contributions to individual differences in rhesus monkey biobehavioral development. In *Perinatal development: A psychobiological perspective* ed. N. Krasnegor, E. Blass, M. Hofer, & W. Smotherman. New York: Academic Press.

Suomi, S. J. (In press). Primate separation models of affective disorders. In *Adaption, learning, and affect*, ed. J. Madden. New York: Raven Press.

Suomi, S. J., and Harlow, H. F. (1975). The role and reason of peer friendships in rhesus monkeys. In *Friendships and peer relations*, ed. M. Lewis and L. Rosenblum. New York: John Wiley & Sons.

Suomi, S. J. and Harlow, H. F. (1978). Early experience and social development in rhesus monkeys. In *Social and personality development*. In ed. M. Lamb. New York: Holt, Rinehart & Winston.

Chapter 4

Theoretical Issues in Investigating Intellectual Plasticity

Sandra Scarr

If one is to understand how genetic and environmental factors interact in human development, producing both individual variability as well as species-typical features, one must grapple theoretically with two quite different perspectives in psychology. Until recently the major purpose of most developmental psychologists' research was the discovery of universal laws of human behavior. In principle, such laws would apply to all of the people all of the time. At the same time a much smaller group of developmental psychologists focused their research on the study of individual differences, particularly individual responses to life events. The history of the two orientations can be traced to what Cronbach (1957) called the two disciplines of scientific psychology, to wit, nomothetic research on species-typical or average trends in human behavior and research on individual differences. Today the two disciplines are merging as psychologists focus on behavior across the entire life span.

David Buss (1984) outlined the distinctive features of the two disciplines of scientific psychology, which, following Ernst Mayr (1963), he called *typological* and *population* approaches. The former, typological, is concerned primarily with painting the human species in broad strokes. The population approach is more concerned with detecting fine variations within the species. Psychology's two scientific disciplines, to use Cronbach's terms, have their parallel in Mayr's contrast of typological and population approaches in biology. The former is philosophically platonic. Although there are variations within the species, these are really considered imperfect versions of some ideal type. What is important in this view is to understand the true nature of the species or the ideal. Population thinking, however, turns that idea on its head; its philosophical roots are in evolutionary theory. According to this view, species-typical features are strongly canalized, hence highly adaptive, clusters of interrelated characters. However, individual variation must be considered since it is the raw material on which natural selection works. Neither the typological nor the population approach is sufficient for our understanding of human nature and development, but both are necessary for it.

What is needed is an explanatory system rooted firmly in the biological notion of *epigenesis*. The explanatory system should emphasize the ways in which genetic and environmental signals interact to produce both species-typical and individual characteristics. The problem is compounded, moreover, by the fact that nomothetic approaches in psychology prefer proximal or efficient causes (in Aristotelian terms), while investigators studying individual differences prefer to focus on ultimate or evolutionary causes (in terms of adaptation). The argument advanced here is that any treatment of human development explaining individual differences must, to be a complete account, incorporate both kinds of causes and specify their relationship. This is the epigenetic approach, which I will illustrate in the present chapter.

A Statement of the Problem

Empirical Evidence

The major question is, How do genetic and environmental causes interact to guide human development? The specific examples discussed here are taken mostly from the study of intellectual development. More research has been concentrated here than in any other area of cognitive development. As a result of these efforts, it is generally understood that for virtually all measures of intellect and personality there is always a higher correlation for parents and their biological offspring than for adopted children. Yet these correlations average only about .50. This fact has led to the notion that genetic and environmental factors provide almost equal weights in guiding developmental progress. As will be shown, however, a careful study of the development of these characteristics over time yields some surprising findings that challenge traditional learning and social learning theories.

Figure 4.1 shows WAIS (Wechsler Adult Intelligence Test) IQ Scores from a study of adolescents who were adopted in infancy. The children's scores were complied during the periods of adolescence and young adulthood (16 to 22 years) and are regressed on the adopted parents' WAIS IQ Scores. The sample consisted of 115 families with two or more adopted children whose education varied from 10 to 20 years of schooling. The children's IQ scores vary from 75 to above 130. The mean IQ score in the sample is 106. As shown, there is very little relationship between adopted children's IQ scores at the end of the child-rearing period (the end of adolescence) and those of their adopted parents.

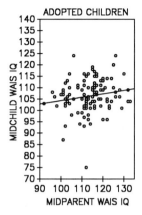

Figure 4.1

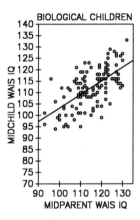

Figure 4.2

Figure 4.2 shows the same data for children reared by biological parents. These families are quite similar to those of the adoptees (major demographic). In this sample the average IQ score is about 116. The sample included parents who varied in educational level from completion of the eighth grade to 19 years of total education. The figure shows the relationship between the WAIS IQ scores of parents and the intellectual outcomes of their children, at least as measured by WAIS IQ scores. There is a significant regression of child's on parent's scores of .64.

Table 4.1 shows the adopted children's WAIS IQ scores regressed on their adoptive parents' IQ scores. There is some slight relationship between the scores, but parents who vary in IQ scores from 90 to over 130 have children whose scores vary from 70 to 130—there is a very slight relationship.

As table 4.1 also shows, there is a substantial relationship between the IQ scores of biological offsprings and the IQ scores of their parents, which again vary across a considerable range. In other words, in these biological families there is a correlation between the average child's IQ and the average parents' IQ of .64, as compared to that with parents' educational level of .38. These relationships are clearly much stronger than for the adoptee's family members.

The same trends are also evident in studies of personality characteristics. Table 4.2 shows data for introversion-extroversion on the Eysenck Personality Inventory. The two major dimensions of the Eysenck Inventory are introversion-extroversion and anxiety or neuroticism. The data reveal little relationship between the scores of adopted parents (who vary across the entire range of scores) and their children (who also vary across the entire range). Thus the parents' extroversion or introversion has apparently little impact on the development of the same personality trait in adopted children. Table 4.2 shows the extroversion data for biological children. Clearly, the relationship between these (personality) variables in biological parents and their offspring is higher than in parents and their adopted children.

The results of studies assessing anxiety are remarkably similar to those obtained in studies of introversion-extroversion. Clearly, information about anxiety levels of adoptive parents provides no basis for

Table 4.1
Correlations of mid parent and mid child IQ scores and parent education

Biological	.38	.64
Adoptive	.14	.18

Table 4.2
Correlations of twins and siblings for personality test scores in
late adolescence

	Twins			Siblings	
	MZ Together	MZ Apart	DZ	Biological	Adopted
Genetic correlation	1.00	1.00	0.50	0.50	0.00
Personality Scale					
Introversion-Extroversion	0.52	0.61	0.25	0.20	0.07
Neuroticism	0.52	0.55	0.22	0.28	0.05
Impulsivity	0.48	—	0.29	0.20	0.05
Median	0.52[a]	0.65[b]	0.25[a]	0.20[c]	0.07[c]

[a] 27 CPI Scales from Nichols (1978)
[b] 11 DPQ Scales from Bouchard (1984) and EPI Scales from Shield (1962)
[c] EPI, DPQ, and APQ scales from Scarr, Webber, Weinberg, and Wittig (1981)

predicting children's anxiety scores. There is, however, a small but significant relationship in the biological families. The personality scales show a weaker relationship between parent and child scores than the intellectual scales.

Theoretical Explanations
The first place to look for explanations for the resemblances between parents and their children is in the effect of families' environments on child development. Measures of the home environment, such as Betty Caldwell and Bob Bradley's home scale (1978) and the family environment scale of Moos and Moss (1981), have been shown to correlate with children's behavioral characteristics, including intelligence and social adjustment. Parents who provide intellectually stimulating homes, who live in communities with good schools, safe streets, and well-behaved peers, are more likely to have more intellectually adept and less delinquent children than parents who provide a less advantaged environment. Thus, generalizations about differences among children reared in different home environments and correlations between parental and child characteristics do seem possible, at least for biological relatives. What is not clear, however, is the nature of the underlying causal sequences.

Theories of family effects on children most often focus on home environments as determinant of children's outcomes. Most psychologists interpret these correlations to mean that the environment provided by the parents both at home and in the larger community cause children to have more favorable or less favorable outcomes. The weakness of this approach is that measures of the home environment almost certainly reflect underlying predispositions of the parent, and these may well have a biological base. As Robert Plomin (1990, 131) stated,

> Two frequently studied dimensions of the family environment are parental love and control. These measures are obviously measures of parental behavior. For example, some parents hug and kiss their children whenever they are within reach. Others rarely display physical affection. Some parents are firm disciplinarians, and others avoid disciplining their children. Parental behavior is also ultimately responsible for the physical features of the family environment. For example, the most widely used environmental item in studies of mental development is the number of books in the home. But books do not magically appear in the shelves— parents usually put them there.

Parental behaviors underlie every aspect of the home environment and many characteristics of the neighborhoods in which children grow up. Child-rearing styles are, after all, parental behaviors. Standards of living depend on parental education, occupational achievements, and family income. Aside from a small minority of families with inherited wealth, the style and advantages of children's environments depend largely on the parents' own characteristics. Parental behaviors are necessarily a function of their own unique gene-environment interactions that produce individual differences in talent, personality, and interests. In other words, parents transmit these characteristics to their children *genetically* as well as through *behavioral interactions.*

For this reason, observed high correlations between parental and home characteristics and children's developmental progress can be taken two ways. They may be evidence for the importance of environmental factors in development; they may also be evidence of the pervasive effects of biologically based predispositions on parenting styles and child-rearing practices. For example, parental education courses are predicated on the notion that parents who know more about child development will treat their children in more benign ways. One might infer from this that there is a causal relationship between such parental training and parental behavior. This "intervention" interpretation also predicts that parents who are ill informed about child development may engage in less benign or constructive parenting strategies, and consequently their children will have poorer outcomes. Richard Weinberg and I (1978) have referred to this prediction as an *intervention fallacy* because we have observed a significant correlation between such parenting characteristics and strategies in *biological relatives.* This suggests that the use of benign, less constructive parenting techniques is at best only partially shaped by formal instruction and/or imitation and has a deeper biological basis as well (see figure 4.3).

Observations from Behavioral Genetics
The merits of several possible theories concerning family resemblances and the effects of parental behavior on child development can be evaluated by considering some data about individual variation in intelligence taken from twin studies in which both genetic and environmental variables can be controlled.

Observation #1   In biologically related families the correlations of late adolescents' and young adult siblings' IQ test scores are approximately .50. In adopted families the IQ correlations for adopted siblings unrelated to each other are 0. In our own studies (Scarr and Weinberg, 1978, 1983) the correlation at an average age of 18 on WAIS IQ scores for our 100 pairs of adopted siblings was − .03. In a very large study of adoptees entering the armed services in Finland the correlation was − .02.

Observation #2   Younger adopted siblings are more similar in intelligence than older adopted siblings. Studies in adopted families where the children's age averages 7 or 8 years and varies between 4 and about 12, the mean correlation for IQ scores of adopted genetically unrelated siblings has ranged from .25 to .39 in five or six studies. For older children no resemblance was observed. For biological siblings the correlation was higher but still considerably less for older than for younger siblings.

Observation #3   In both late adolescence and adulthood monozygotic twins' IQ correlations averaged .85. That is as similar as the same person tested twice on different occasions, whereas the average IQ score for fraternal twins, who are no more alike than biological siblings, is about .55. This correlation is a little bit higher than ordinary siblings but not much. But in infancy and early childhood, monozygotic twins' intellectual correlations still averaged .85. Dyzygotic twins are much more similar in infancy and early childhood than they are in later adolescence and adulthood—the dyzygotic twins' correlations averaged .60 to .75 in infancy and early childhood. These findings raise the question of why people become less and less similar the longer they live together.

Observation #4   Identical twins who have been reared for most or all of their lives in different families resemble each other intellectually to such an extent that their IQ correlations in several well-documented studies average .76. It is also the case that the personality test correlations for identical twins reared mostly apart in different families are higher than those of identical twins reared together. The median correlation on personality scores for identical twins reared apart as reported in several studies is .65. This median correlation has been found in Britain, Denmark, and the United States. For identical twins reared together in the same household all their lives, the average personality test correlations is .55 (cf. Tellegen et al. 1988).

These observations lead many reasonable people to conclude that genetic variation accounts for at least 50 percent of individual differences in IQ and personality test scores. Further, the variations among home environments account for substantial differences in IQ test scores in early development but little or no variation in scores during adolescence and adulthood. These results were obtained on a range of families with average to favorable environments. People who volunteer for family studies are usually working-class to upper-middle-class folk. They tend not to be highly pathological, because really sick people don't volunteer for behavioral science studies. Therefore I must disclaim any generalizations to pathological or sociologically deviant family environments. Nevertheless, even with these caveats it would appear that variation among home environments accounts for a significant amount of variation in child development during infancy and early childhood but contributes little or nothing from adolescence on. Nearly all of the environmental variation in IQ test scores for people reared in adequate to favorable environments arises from differences in the experiences of children within the same family, not between families. This is a surprising result for which traditional learning theory and social learning theories cannot account.

If we accept the notion that genetic variability accounts for at least 50 percent of the variation in intelligence between individuals at adolescence and adulthood, what accounts for the remainder of the variance? This is, after all, not error variance. Rather it represents the effects of differences in the individual experiences of children raised within the same family. As pointed out, these differences are not accounted for by different parenting styles and global family environments.

It is noteworthy that these findings are virtually anomalous for traditional theories emphasizing imitation, role modeling, and simple reinforcement mechanisms. Yet such explanatory systems still tend to be emphasized by developmentalists. Two factors account for this. One is that most studies in developmental psychology do not deal with characteristics such as IQ or introversion, which are relatively stable over the entire life span, but rather with immediate interactional outcomes, which may or may not be direct manifestations of intelligence or personality variables. Second, many investigators simply ignore these observations. Yet it seems inescapable that an adequate and complete theory of development and individual differences must deal with these phenomena.

A Proposed Solution

The challenge for developmental theories is to explain how genetically programmed developmental pathways are affected by specific environments to produce adult human beings displaying species-typical characteristics as well as individually different outcomes.

Behavioral development depends both on the genetic program and on a suitable environment for the expression of our human species-typical program. Differences among people are both genetic and environmental. The process by which these differences arise is called *epigenesis,* and the critical task for developmental theory is to explicate the causal sequences involved (see figure 4.3).

Robert Plomin, John Defries, and John Loehlin (1977) describe three

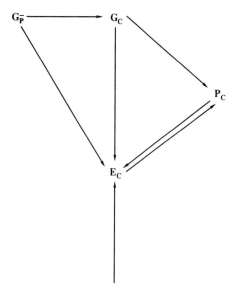

Figure 4.3
A model of behavioral development.
G_P = parental genotype; G_C = child's genotype; E_C = child's environment; P_C = child's phenotype.

mechanisms of epigenetic interaction that address some of these issues directly. This explication involves three propositions:

Proposition #1
The process by which children develop is best described by three kinds of epigenetic programs: (a) a passive kind, in which biological parents provide a rearing environment that is correlated with the genotype of the parent (and hence the child); (b) an evocative kind, in which the child's specific behaviors (based on many personal characteristics) elicit specific feedback from others (positive or negative), which in turn helps to shape behavior (moreover, because each individual expresses different behavioral characteristics, each will evoke a different set of responses from others during the course of development); and (c) an active kind, in which children selectively attend to and selectively learn from aspects of their environment. These selections are presumably based on predispositions with some degree of genetic base and are therefore correlated to some extent with the predispositions and behavioral characteristics of biological relatives.

Proposition #2:
The relative importance of each of these epigenetic programs changes over the course of development. The influence of the passive kind provided by parents wanes over development as children come increasingly into contact with environments and experiences beyond their families (schools, boys' clubs, YMCA's, etc). The importance of the active kind, which involves selecting one's own experiences, increases as we have greater opportunities to select those experiences.

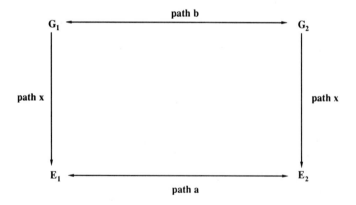

Figure 4.4
A model of environmental similarity based on genetic resemblance.

To be sure, evocative experiences, in which our own behavior elicits feedback from others, continue to operate throughout the life span.

Proposition #3
The degree to which the effects of the environment are experienced differently by each individual increases with development. This proposition is consistent with proposition #2, which predicts a shift from passive to active environmental interaction. Furthermore, this proposition implies that individuals increasingly express unique personality traits as parents come to mediate the child's experiences less through the imposition of their own characteristics.

Insights from Family Research Data
As described, monozygotic twins come to be more similar than dyzygotic ones from infancy on, and biological siblings appear more similar than adopted siblings on almost all measurable characteristics, certainly by the end of adolescence. We have also presented evidence indicating that similarities between both fraternal twins and adopted siblings decline from infancy to adolescence. On the other hand, great similarities exist between identical twins reared even in different homes. These data can be interpreted by the above three propositions.

Table 4.3 provides a set of predictions based on the above explanatory propositions. In effect, this table predicts outcomes at different points in development based on genetic similarity and environmental similarity. For identical twins with perfect genetic correlation, individual experiences will necessarily be very similar. Thus identical twins living in the same family have very similar interests, choices of friends, and food habits. As such, they experience their environments simi-

Table 4.3
The similarity of co-twins and sibling's genotypes and environments for personality

	Genetic Correlation	Correlations in the Environments of Related Pairs	
		Negative Passive Genotype—Environment Effects in Early Development	Active Genotype—Environment Effects in Later Development
MZ twins	1.00	Moderate	High
DZ twins	0.50	Moderate	Moderate
Biological siblings	0.50	Low	Low
Adopted siblings	0.00	Low	Low

larly. This will be true even if identical twins are reared apart, insofar, as they will tend to select and elicit similar experiences and responses to the extent that such opportunities are available. Conversely, adopted siblings reared in the same home, whose genetic correlation is zero, will select and elicit very different experiences, which may not be closely correlated at all. In fact such experiences may well be uncorrelated. This will be even more likely as they get older and are able to control an increasing number of their experiences and personal interactions. Thus adopted siblings may in fact select environments or aspects of environments that are quite uncorrelated, even though they were reared together (see figure 4.4).

Biological siblings and fraternal twins, whose genetic correlations (coefficients of relatedness) are about .50, will be intermediate with respect to the degree of similarity in the experiences they are selecting and eliciting from the environment. Such experiences will become increasingly dissimilar, particularly after they have moved away from their immediate families. This neatly explains why dyzygotic twins and other siblings reared together become increasingly dissimilar as they grow older. Monozygotic twins continue to select and elicit the same experiences from the environment, thereby maintaining the similarities between them.

Enhancing vs. Delaying Environmental Events
Environmental experiences can enhance or delay development for all children as well as generate increased variation in development among children. Again it must be emphasized that the subjects in all groups that we have studied for both the twin and family investigations are living in adequate to favorable environments. Thus these studies cannot shed light on the effects of pathological and/or sociologically deviant environments on development. On the contrary, these studies underscore the notion that given normal nurturance and an adequate environment, individual variability is mainly accounted for by genetic variability and differences in the individual experiences of individuals even within the same environment. On the other hand, there are certain environmental conditions that can and do alter the progress of development for all individuals, regardless of the particular genetic makeup of each. In effect, such environmental events facilitate or retard overall developmental progress regardless of the innate predisposition of each individual. These effects, however, are likely to be small relative to the range of variation within groups. For example, in two studies we found that average IQ scores of adopted children were 106 to 110 (see Scarr and Weinberg 1983). This evidence that adopted children are scoring above the population mean of 101 suggests they

are doing better than they would if they were reared by their natural parents.

This is not an isolated finding. Other studies have found a five to seven IQ point advantage for children reared in enriched environments. I want to stress, however, that correlations between adopted family members are essentially zero at the end of the child-rearing period, while correlations with natural mothers' scores and natural fathers' scores, (to the extent that we have these data) remain higher. Put another way, correlations between children's IQ scores and the educational attainments of natural parents they have never lived with are the same as those of biological parents who reared their own children. The correlation is about .35 in both cases. This suggests that the effects of differences in home environment quality are quite limited. Yet most studies in developmental psychology focus on such factors and interpret differences in the performance of biological relatives as evidence that differences in home environments cause differences in outcomes of children.

It should be stressed that there are macroenvironmental events not necessarily caused by family experiences and characteristics (earthquakes, wars, depression), as well as other large-scale events that affect developmental outcomes. One can also point to events in the lives of individuals that have no relation to personal characteristics (such as accidents), which affect developmental outcomes. Albert Bandura (1982) has pointed to the randomness in life as a factor determining individual progress. On the other hand, the impact of even such large-scale events can be quite different for different people and may well be correlated with other personal characteristics and hence genetic differences as well.

Pertinent to this, Elder, Magruder, and Caspi (1985) have shown that individuals' experiences with the stresses of life during the Depression depended in part on their own individual characteristics. This is consistent with the idea emphasized here: individual cognitive processing and developmental status tend to filter the effects of environmental events and mitigate the effects they exert on developmental progress.

Microenvironments can also exert important effects on development by providing contingencies and structuring sequences of interactions. Some of these are so brief as to go undetected by the participant. A study by Patterson (1988) on aggressive children speaks to this issue eloquently. In this study some parent-child interactions were found to be so rapid and fluid that the participants were virtually unable to code the occurrences as discrete events. It is only through video recording techniques that observers can actually identify the cues projected by the participants. More important, the parents were unaware of the impact of their behaviors on the children. For example, parental retreat in the face of child misbehavior directly contributes to the probability of the misbehavior's recurrence. In such cases the participants may be largely unaware of the effects of their behaviors. Thus they may be powerless to change their behaviors without microcontingency management designed to increase their awareness of what is going on.

It follows, of course, that treatment effectiveness is largely independent of how the child became aggressive in the first place or how the child's aggressiveness has created a family environment of discord and coerciveness. Just as the child's aggresisveness is exacerbated and reinforced by the unfortunate contingency set up in the home, it can be reduced by changing such contingencies. Nevertheless, we cannot ignore the possibility that a genetic predisposition for aggressiveness exists in the child in such cases.

Conclusion

I have argued that to understand development and individuality we need an explanatory system rooted in the biological framework of epigenesis. This explanatory system emphasizes the notion that individuals, to a large extent, determine their own experiences both by selecting and eliciting environmental stimuli. By emphasizing epigenetic processes—interactions between environmental stimuli and inherent predispositions—one presupposes that individuals vary in their susceptibility to environmental events and contingencies. Behaviorist explanations are incomplete because they fail to account for these genetically based developmental processes and cannot explain why different individuals will develop quite different characteristics in virtually identical environments. An adequate theory of development of individual differences must be able to explain these data, including the results discussed here derived from studies of siblings, adoptees, and twins reared in the same families or reared apart.

References

Bandura, A. (1982). The psychology of chance encounters and life paths. *American Psychologist* 37:747–55.

Bouchard, T. J. (1984). Twins reared together and apart: What they tell us about human diversity. In *Individuality and Determinism*, ed. S. W. Fox. New York: Plenum Press.

Buss, D. M. (1984). Evolutionary biology and personality psychology: Toward a conception of human nature and individual differences. *American Psychologist* 39:1135–47.

Caldwell, B. M., and Bradley, R. H. (1978). *Home observation for measurement of the environment.* Little Rock, AR: Caldwell.

Cronbach, L. J. (1957). The two disciplines of scientific psychology. *American Psychologist* 12:671–84.

Elder, G. H., Magruder, T. V., and Caspi, A. (1985). Linking family hardship to children's lives. *Child Development* 56:361–75,

Mayr, E. (1963). *Animal species and evolution.* Cambridge, MA: Belknap Press.

Moos, R. H., and Moss, B. S. (1981). *Family environment scale manual.* Palo Alto, CA: Consulting Psychologists Press.

Patterson, G. R. (1988). Family process: Loops, levels, and linkages. In *Persons In Context: Development Processes,* ed. N. Bolger, A. Caspi, G. Downey, and M. Moorehouse. Cambridge: Cambridge University Press.

Plomin, R. (1990). *Nature and nurture.* Pacific Grove, CA: Brooks/Cole.

Plomin, R., Defries, J. C., and Loehlin, J. C. (1977). Genotype-environment interaction and correlation in the analysis of human behavior. *Psychological Bulletin* 84:309–22.

Scarr, S. (1985). Constructing psychology: Facts and fables for our times. *American Psychologist* 40:499–512.

Scarr, S., and Weinberg, R. A. (1978). The influence of "family background" on intellectual attainment. *American Sociological Review* 43:674–92.

Scarr, S., and Weinberg, R. A. (1983). The Minnesota adoption studies: Malleability and genetic differences. *Child Development* 54:260–7.

Tellegen, A., Lykken, D. T., Bouchard, T. J., and Wilcox, K. J. (1988). Personality similarity in twins reared apart and together. *Journal of Personality and Social Psychology* 54:1031–39.

Chapter 5

Perception, Cognition, and the Ontogenetic and Phylogenetic Emergence of Human Speech

Patricia K. Kuhl

Communication through speech and language is an exclusively human behavior. No other animal's communicative systems parallel the complexity nor the flexibility that is afforded by human language. Man's capacity for language is typically ascribed to specialized abilities that evolved for the processing of linguistic signals. These specialized linguistic abilities are hypothesized to be organized in a processing subsystem that is unique and separate from other cognitive systems. On this view language is "modularized" in an "encapsulated" and "cognitively impenetrable" processing system (Fodor 1983; Liberman and Mattingly 1985).

An alternative view is that language, and all other higher cognitive functions, are subserved by a common underlying architecture (Anderson 1983). This position attempts to formulate a unified theory of mind by asserting that all higher order cognitive functions use similar structure and similar processing strategies rather than ones that are unique and separate. On this view cognition and language deploy the same "distributed" neural machinery that interconnects diverse parts of the brain and serves many purposes (Rummelhart and McClelland 1986; Anderson 1988).

These two views of language, one holding that language stems from a fully encapsulated and independent *module,* and the other that it stems from a more generic and distributed *neural network,* are linked to different perspectives on the phylogenetic evolution of man's capacity for language. Chomsky (1980), a proponent of the modular view, argues that language is the canonical example of a sudden emergence or mutation that brought forward a fully formed and com-

Edited from a paper presented at the Biennial Distinguished Lecture Series, sponsored by the Program for Developmental Research at the University of Maryland. The preparation of this manuscript was supported by grants from NIH (HD 18286, HD 22514, and NS 26521). The author thanks A. N. Meltzoff for comments on an earlier draft of the manuscript.

plex ability. Chomsky argues that until we understand how such mutations can occur, we will not fully comprehend the evolutionary biology of human language. Proponents of the alternative position argue that, regardless of its complexity, language evolved gradually from preexisting abilities (Lieberman 1984; in press). This position favors continuity in the theory of human evolution and suggests that the substrates of language are rooted in nonhuman primates.

These two views offer distinct positions on the ontogeny of language. The first view, that language is a modularized system, holds that humans' linguistic abilities are innate, that the human infant enters the world equipped with mechanisms specially evolved for the processing of linguistic signals. In effect, this view holds that infants are born with a speech module already in place (Fodor 1983; Liberman and Mattingly 1985). The alternative view suggests that infants are highly skilled at birth but that the sophistication with which they approach the acquisition of language stems from more general perceptual and cognitive abilities. On this view infants are initially capable of perceiving complex events and imposing structure on those events. Thus, while holding that infants are quite competent at birth, this position asserts that the infants' competence may well be quite general (Kuhl 1986).

The phonetic level of language—the consonants and vowels that constitute human speech—offers an ideal linguistic signal with which to test hypotheses about the phylogeny and ontogeny of the human capacity for language. The perception of speech sounds can be studied in human infants only a few hours old, well before more formal evidence of language (such as infants' first words) begins to appear. One can also examine the abilities of nonhuman animals to perceive speech sounds. No nonhuman animals are capable of human speech, in part because they lack the supralaryngeal vocal tract that is required to produce speech sounds (Lieberman 1984). The assumption made by many is that animals also have a corresponding lack of the mechanisms involved in the *perception* of speech sounds (Liberman, Mattingly, and Turvey 1972). If this were so, it would provide some evidence of human uniqueness in processing linguistic (phonetic) signals. The goal of the research reviewed here was to make direct comparisons between the speech-perception capabilities of human infants and those of nonhuman animals. By examining the set of behaviors evidenced by both groups and pinpointing where they diverge, we hoped to make inferences about the origins of human infants' abilities and to identify what, if anything, makes them unique. This in turn contributes to the more general question of the evolution of language.

The Development of Vocal Communication

Infants of many animal species are specially sensitive to the vocal signals that are critical to their survival (see Dooling and Hulse 1989 for review). Evolution also seems to have guaranteed human infants' attentiveness to their own species' communications signals. Just as the bat, the bird, the cricket, and the frog are perceptually prepared for the acquisition of species-typical vocal signals, the human baby appears to be extraordinarily well prepared to respond to the human face and the human voice. Evidence supporting interest in the face comes from studies showing that young infants prefer to look at faces rather than at other visual configurations (Frantz and Fagan 1975; Kagan et al. 1966). More surprisingly, studies show that even newborns will imitate facial actions presented to them by their conspecifics (Meltzoff and Moore 1977; 1983; 1989). In one study it was demonstrated that infants as young as 42 minutes old can imitate gestures such as mouth opening and tongue protrusion (Meltzoff and Moore 1983), thus showing that such matching behavior is part of man's basic biological endowment. This extraordinary sensitivity to human facial actions has implications for the evolution of social and communicative development as described by Meltzoff (1988).

My own work has demonstrated the human infant's exquisite sensitivity to human speech. For example, recent work in my laboratory shows that when given a choice among sounds, young infants prefer to listen to "Motherese," a highly melodic speech signal that adults use when addressing infants (Fernald 1985; Grieser and Kuhl 1988; Papousek and Papousek 1981). It is not the syntax or semantics of Motherese that holds infants' attention—it is the acoustic signal itself. When the syntax and semantics of Motherese are stripped away and only the pitch contour of Motherese remains, infants still demonstrate the preference (Fernald and Kuhl 1987). Moreover, the prosodic features of Motherese, its higher pitch, slower tempo, and expanded intonation contours, appear to be universal across language (Fernald and Simon 1984; Grieser and Kuhl 1988). We do not know what makes mothers (fathers too) speak to their infants in this way, but we do know that mothers in every language we have examined thus far produce this kind of speech and that babies demonstrate a preference for it.

The study of Motherese emphasizes the obvious impact of speech on infants' social and affective development. Infants seemingly complete absorbtion with the sound of human speech raises a different question in my mind: Does speech have any linguistic impact on infants?

I was intrigued by the problem of speech acquisition and the sudden onset of "canonical babbling" at about 6 to 8 months of life, regardless of the language environment in which the child was being reared. It caused me to wonder what went on before the onset of speech production. Were infants in any sense processing speech perceptually in a way that had linguistic relevance, even before they could produce speech? And if so, did infants' speech processing depend on listening to the sounds of their native language?

The first study published on speech perception in infants addressed this question. It demonstrated that infants exhibited a phenomenon called *categorical perception* (Eimas et al. 1971). These data provided the first evidence that infants were processing speech sounds in a linguistically relevant manner.

The Phenomenon of Categorical Perception

The phenomenon of categorical perception had been demonstrated in adults by Liberman and his colleagues at Haskins Laboratories in the 1960s (Liberman et al. 1967). Tests of categorical perception used speech sounds created by a computer. The computer created a series of sounds by altering some acoustic variable in small steps. On one end of the series the sounds were identified as the syllable /ba/; on the other end of the continuum the sounds were identified as /pa/ (figure 5.1).

The test involved asking listeners to identify each one of the sounds in the series. Researchers expected that the sounds in the series would be perceived as changing gradually from /ba/ to /pa/, with many sounds in the middle of the series sounding ambiguous. But that is not what happened. Adults reported hearing a series of /ba/s that abruptly changed to a series of /pa/s. There was no in-between. And when researchers asked listeners if they could hear the difference between two adjacent /ba/s (or/pa/s) in the series, they could not do so, even though the two /ba/s (or /pa/s) were physically different. Listeners did not hear differences between adjacent stimuli in the series until they heard a big change—the change from /ba/ to /pa/. The fact that listeners' responses were "categorical" gave the phenomenon its name.

Further research on categorical perception in adults revealed that the phenomenon was sensitive to the linguistic environment and experience of the listener (Miyawaki et al. 1975). It occurred only for sounds in an adult's native language. For example, when Japanese listeners were tested on a series of sounds that ranged from /ra/ to /la/ for American listeners, a distinction that is not phonemic in Japanese, they did not hear a sudden change at the boundary between /ra/ and /la/. They heard no change at all. (This is why Japanese speak-

An Acoustic Continuum
with Equal Physical Steps

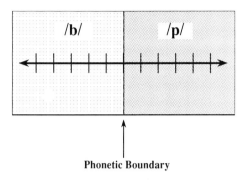

Phonetic Boundary

Figure 5.1
Illustration of the *categorical perception* phenomenon. An acoustic continuum is created in which changes in a physical dimension are made in small, physically equal steps. Perception of the stimuli on the continuum does not change gradually in accordance with the change in the physical dimension. Rather the stimuli are heard as a series of /ba/s that changes abruptly at the phonetic boundary to a series of /pa/s.

ers substitute /l/ for /r/ in speech—*flied lice* for *fried rice*.) American listeners reported hearing a series of /ra/s that changed suddenly to a series of /la/s, just as they had with the /ba/ and /pa/ stimuli.

The finding that categorical perception was language specific suggested that it was probably learned through exposure to a specific language. This is what Eimas had set out to test in 1971. The question was: What would very young infants hear when presented with a series of /ba/s and /pa/s or /ra/s and /la/s? If hearing the sudden shift in the stimuli at the boundary between two categories was the result of experience with language (perhaps as a result of hearing their parents contrast words containing /b/ and /p/— such as *bat* and *pat*—then young infants would not be expected to show it. Older infants, on the other hand, who had experienced language, might show the categorical perception phenomenon.

Infants' responses to the sounds were monitored using a specially designed technique that relied on the measurement of sucking (Eimas et al. 1971). The results of the study revealed that infants demonstrated categorical perception. Moreover, infants demonstrated the phenomenon not only for the sounds of their own native language but also for sounds from foreign languages (Streeter 1976; Lasky, Syrdal-Lasky, and Klein 1975; Aslin et al. 1981). In all cases, infants reacted to the sounds as though they heard a sudden shift in the series at the adult-defined boundary between the two phonetic categories. Infants appeared to be born multilingual, at least as far as phonetic perception was concerned.

Comparative Studies On Speech Perception

When the report from Eimas's lab was published, I had been reading about work on the cross-fostering of infant chimps by human adults (Gardner and Gardner 1990). It became clear from early work on cross-fostering that chimps could not learn to articulate human speech. Their vocal tracts and oral structures did not allow them to produce speech (Lieberman 1984). My question was whether animals' inability to produce speech was paralleled on the perception side. Were animals also unable to *perceive* human speech? That is, would nonhuman animals fail to demonstrate speech phenomena, such as categorical perception, that human adults and infants succeeded in demonstrating?

I began to study how nonhuman animals perceived speech sounds. The initial tests focused on the categorical perception effect (Kuhl and Miller 1975). We wanted to know whether animals heard a sudden shift in a series of stimuli at the location (for humans) of the phonetic boundary between two categories, just as humans did. Our first study resembled an identification test like those used with adult human listeners, only our test was conducted with an animal, the chinchilla (Kuhl and Miller 1975). In later tests I studied monkeys (Kuhl and Padden 1982, 1983). Both animals exhibit very good hearing and are often used in experiments on hearing because their hearing is similar to man's.

In the initial study (Kuhl and Miller 1975), animals were trained to respond differentially to computer-synthesized versions of the syllables /da/ and /ta/. The two stimuli were the endpoints of a series of stimuli that were identified (by human listeners) as /da/s and /ta/s. To one of the endpoint stimuli animals were trained to jump across a midline barrier in a cage. To the other stimulus the animal was trained to inhibit the crossing response, and this was rewarded. When performance on the endpoints was near perfect, the intermediate stimuli—those between the /da/ and /ta/ endpoints—were tested.

The critical trials were those in which intermediate stimuli were tested. The animals had not had any previous training on these stimuli and were given no feedback during the test. Each stimulus was presented and the animals' responses were monitored. These stimuli were the ones of greatest importance for theory because there were no clues telling the animal how to respond to them. The question was: How would animals partition the continuum—would they hear the same kind of quantum leap from one category to another that humans do? None of the training they were given gave them any clue to where to draw the boundaries.

Figure 5.2 displays the results of this study (Kuhl and Miller 1975). As the data show, animals also appeared to hear the abrupt shift in the stimuli—and it occurred at precisely the location where human adults separate the /da/ and /ta/ categories. Subsequent tests on a series of stimuli ranging from /ba/ to /pa/, and tests on a series ranging from /ga/ to /ka/, were then conducted (Kuhl and Miller 1978). In all cases, the animals responded as though they heard a sudden change in the speech stimuli at the exact location where human adults perceived a shift from one phonetic category to another (see Kuhl 1986 for review).

We had thus provided some evidence supporting the evolutionary continuity hypothesis. We had shown that this aspect of the perception of human speech did not separate man from other animals. On the basis of these findings, we speculated that the boundaries for other phonetic categories might coincide with animals' *natural psychophysical boundaries*. Additional experiments were conducted to test this, our hypothesis was strongly supported (see Kuhl 1988 for review). The categorical perception of speech sounds was thus not unique to human beings.

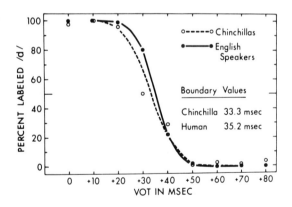

Figure 5.2
Chinchillas were trained to respond differentially to the endpoint stimuli on a continuum ranging from /da/ to /ta/. Once they were trained, the intermediate stimuli were presented and no feedback was given. The data show the mean percentage of "/d/" responses by chinchillas and humans. The phonetic boundaries between the two speech categories for the two species do not differ significantly. (From Kuhl and Miller 1978).

Infants' Perception of Speech: Beyond Categorical Perception?

Given that the phenomenon of categorical perception did not separate man from other animals, I began looking at more complex behaviors in human infants, hoping to find a place where the two species would diverge. Since that time my colleagues and I have produced four new findings on human infants' responses to speech. In one case repeated tests have failed to find the phenomenon in animals. In the other two cases we suspect that animals may not demonstrate the behaviors, but we have not as yet conducted the relevant tests.

The first phenomenon is a demonstration of *talker normalization* in infants (Kuhl 1979a, 1983). Our studies show that infants perceive vowel sounds produced by many different talkers as belonging to the same category. Why is that surprising? As adults we have no problem perceiving that a word produced by different talkers—a simple word such as *peep* produced by a man, a woman, and a child—is the same word; why is it surprising that an infant might do the same? It is surprising that infants do this because it requires a normalization process. Computers, for example, have a great deal of difficulty classifying words correctly when they are produced by a wide variety of different talkers (Kuhl et al. 1989). Yet, at least by 6 months of age, human infants accomplish this feat.

The second phenomenon focuses on the underlying basis of infants' categorization abilities. Our recent findings suggest that as early as 6 months of age, infants organize speech categories around an exemplar that adults consider to be a particularly good instance of the category, a prototype of the category (Grieser and Kuhl 1989; Kuhl in press).

The third phenomenon goes beyond the auditory processing of speech signals. This phenomenon has to do with infants' cross-modal (auditory-visual) perception of speech. We show that infants can detect correspondences between auditory speech signals and the visible articulatory movements that typically accompany them—a phenomenon linked to lip-reading (Kuhl and Meltzoff 1982, 1984a).

The fourth phenomenon is vocal imitation. Imitation examines the link between the perception and the production of speech. When infants imitate speech, they demonstrate connections between auditory perception and articulatory movements that enable them to produce speech themselves (Kuhl and Meltzoff 1982, 1988). Vocal imitation is essential to the development of speech.

Talker Normalization

The first phenomenon—talker normalization—requires what cognitive psychologists call categorization—the ability to render discriminably different things equivalent (Bruner, Goodnow, and Austin 1956).

Categorization is a phenomenon that characterizes all of perception. As stimuli typically vary along many dimensions, categorization requires that we recognize similarities in the presence of considerable variance. Often the exact criteria used to categorize are not obvious. Consider the categories *cat* and *dog*. Describing what distinguishes them, and thus what uniquely categorizes them, is not simple. They both have two eyes, four legs, fur, a tail, and so on. Configurational properties of the face probably distinguish them, but trying to describe these features is difficult. Yet we would not expect an adult to mistakenly identify a cat as a dog, or vice versa.

In speech a similar categorization problem exists. Take a simple example, such as the vowel categories /a/ as in *cot* and /ae/ as in *cat*. The differences between the two vowels are not subtle to the human ear; they are clearly different. But trying to program a computer to identify these vowels correctly when they are spoken by different individuals demonstrates it to be a very difficult program.

Figure 5.3 provides a schematic illustration of the talker normalization problem. When a single talker produces different vowels (left panel), the vowels are easily separable on some acoustic basis. The circles for each vowel enclose the utterances produced by that talker

The Talker Normalization Problem

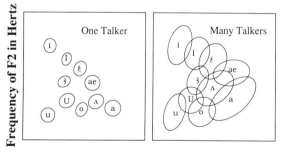

Frequency of F1 in Hertz

Figure 5.3
Schematic diagram illustrating the problem of talker normalization. When a single talker produces different vowels (left panel), the formant frequencies of different vowels do not overlap. However, when many talkers produce the vowels (right panel), the values of the formants for adjacent vowels overlap a great deal, making it difficult to specify the acoustic values that define any one particular vowel.

at different times. As shown, there is variability, but the circles do not overlap with one another. But when many different talkers produce vowels (right panel), there is overlap in the physical cues that underlie the two categories, and the circles overlap with one another. The explanation for this has to do with the fact that people with different-sized vocal tracts (males, females, and children) produce different resonant frequencies when they create the same mouth shape. Thus far no one has successfully described an algorithm that correctly recovers which of the vowels a speaker produced when acoustic information (the formant frequency values) is the only thing provided. In humans, various attempts to explain the processes by which we normalize the speech produced by different talkers have been offered; most of them involve computation of some kind (see Lieberman 1984 for review).

The critical question for the current discussion is whether infants recognize equivalence when the same vowel is produced by different talkers. Are all /a/s the same to the baby, regardless of the talker who produced them? It is of no small import to the child that such an ability exists early in life. Vocal-tract normalization is critical to the infant's acquisition of speech. Their vocal tracts cannot produce the frequencies produced by the adult's vocal tract, so they could not mimic the exact frequencies that an adult produces. Infants must normalize speech perceptually in order to imitate it productively.

In order to test infants' talker normalization abilities, we used a simple procedure that is shown in figure 5.4. The infant sits on a parent's lap and is visually engaged by an assistant who manipulates toys silently. A speech sound, such as the vowel sound /a/, plays repeatedly from the loudspeaker at the infant's left. The infant quickly learns that when the sound changes from the vowel /a/ to the vowel /i/ a bear playing a drum inside a black box on top of the loudspeaker is turned on. This head-turning response is the conditioned response used to test the infant's ability to normalize speech.

Once trained, the infant produces head-turning responses only when /i/ vowels occur and does not turn during presentations of the vowel /a/. The experimental question is: What will infants do when they are presented with new instances of /a/ and /i/ vowels, instances clearly different from the /a/ and /i/ stimuli heard during training? If young infants are capable of talker normalization—if they hear all /a/s (or all /i/s) as belonging to the same category—then their initial training to respond to a single /i/ sound should generalize to all members of the category. By this hypothesis, an infant trained to produce a head turn to the male's /i/ vowel, but not to his /a/ vowel, should produce head

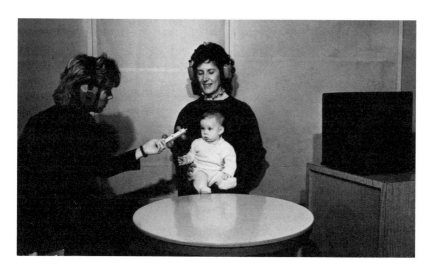

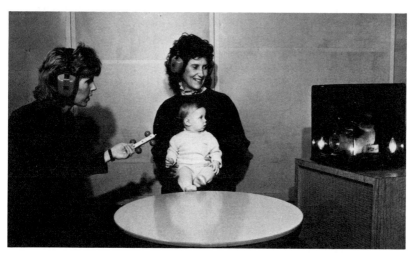

Figure 5.4
The procedure used to test infants' perception of speech. Infants who sit on a parent's lap watch toys held by an assistant (top panel). They are trained to produce a head-turning response toward the loudspeaker (located at the infant's left) when one speech sound, repeated as a background stimulus, is changed to a new speech sound. If the infant produces a head-turning response at the appropriate time, a visual reinforcer (an animated toy animal) is activated (bottom panel). The procedure is used to test infants' abilities to categorize novel speech stimuli. (See text for further details.)

turns to all novel /i/s (ones produced by females or children), but not to equally novel /a/s.

The results demonstrated that the hypothesis of talker normalization or phonetic categorization was correct (Kuhl 1979a). Infants responded correctly to the novel vowels. If the infant had been trained to turn to the male's /a/, then all novel /a/s evoked the response, while very few of the novel /i/s did. The same was true if infants were trained to turn to the male's /i/—all novel /i/s evoked the response. Figure 5.5 shows the percent head-turning responses to all of the stimuli introduced in the experiment. In the top panel infants' responses to the two stimuli used during the training phase are shown. In the bottom panel infants' responses to the stimuli presented during the test phase of the experiment are shown. Each bar in the bottom panel represents the infants' responses to the utterances of a particular talker; each talker produced one token from category 1 and one token from category 2.

As shown, infants sorted the stimuli by phonetic class, regardless of the talker producing the sounds. Infants produced high numbers of head-turning responses to the novel stimuli that were members of the phonetic category to which they were initially trained to respond (category 1 stimuli). They produced very few head-turning responses to equally novel stimuli that were members of the second phonetic category (category 2). An analysis of infants' first-trial responses showed that infants performed correctly on the very first trial. These results suggest that 6-month-old infants categorize all /a/s (and all /i/s) as the same—they appear to be capable of normalizing the speech produced by different talkers.

Kuhl (1983) extended these results to vowel categories that are much more similar from an acoustic standpoint and therefore much more difficult to categorize. The vowels were synthesized versions of /a/ (as in *cot*) and /ɔ/ (as in *caught*). In naturally produced words containing these vowels the overlap in the first two formant frequencies is so extensive that the two categories cannot be separated on this acoustic dimension (Peterson and Barney 1952). Moreover, in most dialects used in the United States talkers do not distinguish between the two vowels.

The experiment was run just as before. Infants were trained on the /a/ and /ɔ/ vowels spoken by a male talker. Then novel vowels spoken by female and child talkers, with additional random changes in the pitch contours of these vowels, were introduced. Results of the /a– / study demonstrated that infants could still categorize the novel vowels correctly (Kuhl 1983). However, the results also showed that the task was difficult and suggested that when speech categories are very

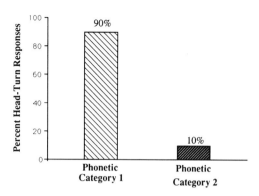

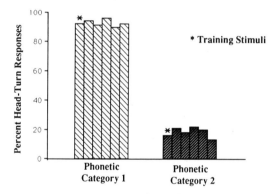

Figure 5.5
The results of tests on infants' abilities to categorize speech sounds. Infants were trained to produce a head-turning response to a single vowel from one phonetic category (either /a/ or /i/) produced by a male speaker, while refraining from producing the head-turning response to the opposite vowel produced by that same talker (top panel). Once trained, the infants' tendencies to produce the head-turning response to novel stimuli produced by men, women, and children from the /a/ and /i/ categories were tested (bottom panel). Infants' head-turning responses demonstrated that they perceptually sorted the novel stimuli by phonetic class.

similar, there is a cognitive cost associated with categorizing speech when the talker is constantly changed.

We pursued this issue further, making the experiment harder still by using many more talkers and close vowels—the /a/ in *pot* vs. the /ae/ in *pat*. This time we used vowels produced by 12 different men, women, and children. The vowels were produced naturally, rather than being computer generated, as they had been in the previous studies. We purposely chose voices that sounded very different so that extracting a constant vowel would be especially difficult. We used male talkers with deep voices, women with exceptionally high voices, even people with colds who sounded very nasal but could be understood. Adults could classify the sounds accurately. What about babies?

Figure 5.6 displays the performance on both the two training stimuli (top panel), and on the test stimuli. The results revealed two things. First, infants can categorize vowels by phonetic class when the talker is constantly changing. As shown, the percentage of head turns to novel stimuli from the two categories differed greatly. But there was another interesting finding. Although infants succeeded, the task was difficult. Switching attention from one talker to another while categorizing two vowels had a cognitive cost associated with it. These data are interesting because they are similar to data on adults showing that there are increased processing demands associated with a change in the talker producing a set of words (Mullennix and Pisoni 1990; Mullennix, Pisoni, and Martin 1989). Moreover, infants' performance on individual tokens varied. Some were classified more accurately than the training token, even though they were completely novel. Thus we had found two things. First, infants at a very young age were capable of talker normalization well before the age at which they passed any milestones in the production or in the comprehension of speech. And second, categorization of exemplars varied. Some novel instances were easier to classify than others.

This second finding came as somewhat of a surprise. Studies of categorical perception had led us to believe that, at least for speech, all members of a given category were equivalent. But these studies had been done with synthesized utterances in which all the acoustic parameters that indicate gender and those that signal a specific talker had been removed. Our studies with natural speech were replete with variation—people who were old and young, big and small, with and without colds, and all of these things led to differences in the signal that had to be contended with in the categorization task. This led to a new suggestion—that the members of a phonetic category varied qualitatively and that some might be better exemplars than others.

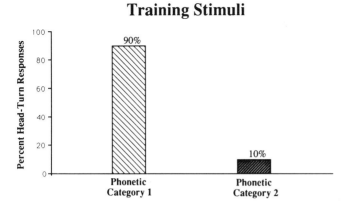

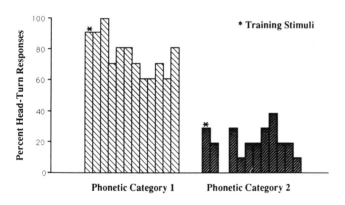

Figure 5.6
The results of tests on infants' abilities to categorize speech sounds. Infants were trained to produce a head-turning response to a single vowel from one phonetic category (either /a/ or /i/) produced by a male speaker, while refraining from producing the head-turning response to the opposite vowel produced by that same talker (top panel). Once trained, the infants' tendencies to produce the head-turning response to novel vowels produced by twelve different men, women, and children were tested (bottom panel). Infants sorted novel stimuli from the two vowel categories by phonetic class, suggesting that they *normalize* the speech produced by different talkers.

Speech Prototypes

There was some evidence in the literature that certain consonants were better exemplars than others and that they led to increased effects in certain perceptual tasks (Miller 1977; Miller and Volaitis 1989; Samuel 1982). We decided to pursue the idea that certain stimuli served as *prototypes* for speech categories. We began a new line of studies on the underlying basis of speech categorization. Our results suggest that adults and even infants organize vowel categories around an exceptionally good instance—a prototype of the category (Grieser and Kuhl 1989; Kuhl in press).

Rosch (1975) has described prototypes for physical objects as the best members of the category, the ones most representative of the category as a whole. A robin is a prototype of the category *bird*. An ostrich is not. Prototypes appear to be perceptually special. They are often processed more quickly, are more easily remembered, and are frequently preferred over others. Our question was whether there were preferred instances (prototypes) for speech categories, and if so, whether those stimuli served as cognitive reference points for speech categories.

To test the prototype hypothesis for speech, we synthesized many different instances of /i/—nearly a hundred, covering the entire range of formant values typically seen in adult speakers. We then asked adults to judge the relative goodness of each of the vowels using a scale from 1 to 7. A "7" indicated a particularly good exemplar—a perfect /i/. A "1" indicated an /i/, but a very poor one. Adults' ratings were very consistent. There was a certain location in the /i/ vowel space that always resulted in better ratings. As you moved away from that spot, the ratings became consistently worse—so adults did not perceive all members of a vowel category as equivalent. Some instances were better than others. Given that some were more striking, what was the perceptual consequence?

We developed two hypotheses. The first was that the prototype /i/ would be perceived by adults to be more similar to other /i/ vowels than the nonprototype, because it was more representative of the category as a whole. The second hypothesis added a developmental dimension. We wondered whether young infants would behave differently in a categorization test when presented with a prototype, as opposed to a nonprototype, vowel.

Two /i/ vowels were chosen from the set we had had rated by adults, one given the highest rating on average—a 6.8, and another one given a relatively poor rating— a 1.7. It is important to note that both the good and the poor exemplar were always rated as an /i/ rather than some other vowel. Both were /i/s, but the one with the 6.8 rating was perceived to be a better instance of /i/. We then computer synthesized a number of variants of /i/ around both of these two vowels.

Figure 5.7 displays the stimuli used in the experiment (Kuhl in press). Each circle on the diagram indicates an instance of a vowel. There are 32 stimuli around the prototype, represented by open circles, and 32 around the nonprototype, represented by closed circles. They form four rings around the center stimulus. An important factor about these rings is that the stimuli on them were scaled using the *mel scale* (Stevens in press). The psychophysical particulars of this scale aren't critical, but its function is to equate the distance between the center stimuli and the surrounding stimuli for the two groups (Kuhl in press). The stimuli on the first ring around the prototype are scaled to be just as discriminable from the prototype as the stimuli on the first ring around the nonprototype are from the nonprototype. One other thing to note about the stimuli is that the variants on one vector were included in both sets of stimuli. The perception of these stimuli is par-

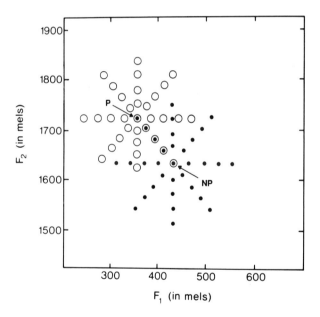

Figure 5.7
Stimuli used to test the speech prototype phenomenon. Two vowels from the /i/ vowel category were chosen, one judged by adults to be a particularly "good instance" from the category (the prototype, shown as P), and the other judged to be an /i/ with a relatively poor goodness rating (the nonprototype, shown as NP). Around each of these two stimuli, 32 variants were created by manipulating the first two formant frequencies. The stimuli were scaled using the mel scale (see text for details).

ticularly interesting because both groups of subjects were tested on them.

The hypothesis was that the prototype would be perceived as more similar to its surrounding variants than the nonprototype would be to its surrounding variants. That is, listeners would need to go further away from the prototype before they heard a difference between it and its variants than would be true of the nonprototype, even though distance was psychophysically controlled.

Two groups of 6-month-old infants were tested. The head-turning task was used. Infants heard either the prototype or the nonprototype as the reference sound during the experiment. We tested discrimination of the center stimulus from each of the surrounding stimuli and measured generalization of the head-turning response from the center stimulus to the surrounding stimuli (Kuhl in press).

We predicted that both groups, the prototype and the nonprototype, would show an effect of distance; that is, for each group, generalization from the center stimulus to the surrounding variants would be highest for those variants nearest the center vowel (those on the first ring), and generalization would decrease as you moved further away from it. This is straightforward stimulus generalization. But the prototype hypothesis predicted something more. It predicted that there would also be a significant group effect. We expected that infants in the prototype group would produce higher generalization scores at each distance because the prototype would act as a perceptual magnet and make its surrounding variants be perceived as more similar to it.

Figure 5.8 shows the mean generalization scores for each group for each ring surrounding the center vowel. As shown, there is an effect of distance for each of the two groups. Generalization scores decrease as you move further away from the center vowel. But there is also a group effect. Infants in the prototype group (the dashed line) had higher generalization scores at *each* distance. They treated many of the variants surrounding the prototype as indistinguishable from it. Infants in the nonprototype group did this to a much lesser degree. A two-way ANOVA (Analysis of Variance) examining the effect of group (prototype and nonprototype) and distance (levels 1 to 4) on infants' generalization scores showed that both of the main effects were highly significant (Kuhl in press).

There are two other results that are of interest. First, we correlated adults' ratings of the vowels' goodness for stimuli around the prototype with infants' generalization scores for stimuli around the prototype. The correlation was .95 (Kuhl in press). This suggests that the

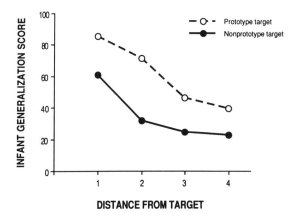

Figure 5.8
Data from a test of speech prototypes in infants. Generalization from the prototype and the nonprototype to surrounding variants (see stimuli in figure 7). Both groups show an effect of distance from the center stimulus, with generalization greater for stimuli near the center stimulus (distance 1) and poorer for stimuli far away from the center stimulus (distance 4). In addition there was an effect of stimulus group. Infants in the prototype group showed greater generalization at each distance when compared to infants in the nonprototype group.

adults' judgment of what constitutes a good or prototypic /i/ versus a nonprototypic /i/ is very closely matched to that of the 6-month-olds.

Second, recall that there was a shared vector that both groups had been tested on (figure 7). Both groups were tested on the stimuli located on the vector between the prototype and the nonprototype. The only difference was whether infants were listening to the prototype and generalizing in the direction of the nonprototype or listening to the nonprototype and generalizing in the direction of the prototype. Infants listening to the prototype generalized as far out as the third ring, whereas infants listening to the nonprototype generalizing in the direction of the prototype failed to generalize as soon as they passed the first ring. In other words, there is directional asymmetry in perception for stimuli on the common vector. This epitomizes the effect. Stimuli appear to be perceptually assimilated by the prototype. I would say that the prototype functions like a perceptual magnet—it draws other stimuli toward it, effectively reducing the perceptual distance between it and the stimuli that surround it.

These data support the notion first expressed by Stevens (1972, 1981), who argued that vowel categories were organized so as to take advantage of the quantal nature of perception. They suggest that some points in vowel space are ideal candidates for category centers, because they are associated with perceptual stability over a broad array of category variants. Other points in vowel space are poor candidates, as perception is not stable and generalization to novel exemplars is weak. The phenomenon is consistent with prototype theory (Medin and Barsalou 1987; Rosch 1975) and is the first data that we are aware of that suggest that infants' speech categories demonstrate internal structure and organization.

The findings raise interesting questions: What makes a particular vowel a prototype? Is there some way of defining the stimulus properties of these ideal vowels? And of more interest to those of us who are attempting to explain development, how do 6-month-old babies know which vowels are prototypes? How do these ideal exemplars get into the mind of the baby?

There are two potential answers to the developmental question, and they make different predictions about the nature of the prototype. The first answer regarding development is that the prototype effect is innate. We may have tapped Platonic ideals. An alternative is that the vowel prototypes are attributable to linguistic input–that infants have already begun to form representations of the vowels in the ambient language, and they summarize this input in terms of the prototype. This second view takes the spoken language of the parents, which is still meaningless to a 6-month-old, as salient input that bathes the baby many hours a day and alters his or her perceptual space.

The two models make different predictions about infants' perception of vowels from a foreign language. The first hypothesis—that vowel prototypes are fixed—predicts that the prototype effect would exist for many vowels, even those that infants have never heard, perhaps all the vowels of all languages. The second hypothesis predicts that the prototype effect would result only when vowels in the infant's own language were used.

To test this hypothesis I designed a cross-language study wherein infants from two different language environments, English and Swedish, are each tested on the English /i/ vowel prototype and also on a prototype of the Swedish front rounded vowel (/y/ in Fant's 1973 notation). The vowel systems of the two languages are very different (Fant 1973), and adults from the two cultures rate the goodness of the exact same vowels very differently. Vowel /i/ prototypes are located in different places for American and Swedish adults, so that an English /i/ prototype is not perceived as a prototype to adult Swedes, and the Swedish /y/ prototype is not perceived as a prototype to adult Americans.

The goal is to conduct an identical study (testing both English and Swedish vowel prototypes) in two different countries. In order to achieve a situation in which an experiment conducted in two different countries was identical, I packed up my entire laboratory (everything—computer, loudspeaker, cables, reinforcers, everything down to the scissors), as well as my research team, which consisted of three testers, and sent them off to Stockholm, Sweden. All aspects of the study remained the same—the testers, the stimuli, the equipment, the reinforcers, the toys used to distract the infants, even the table mothers sat at—the only variable that changed was the language experience of the 6-month-olds who were tested. The question is, Will the 6-month-olds from the two countries resemble their adult counterparts, showing the prototype effect only for the vowels of their own language? Or will vowel prototypes be exhibited universally by infants from both cultures, in the absence of experience?

We are still in the process of testing the infants, so we do not yet know what the answer is, but there is another set of data that is relevant. A test of speech prototypes in my monkey lab has just been completed (Kuhl in press). The results showed that monkeys do *not* show the prototype effect. The test was conducted in a very similar way, the only exception being that monkeys responded by hitting a telegraph key and were reinforced with a squirt of applesauce. The results showed that monkeys demonstrated a significant *distance* effect. In other words, they demonstrated straightforward stimulus generalization around both the prototype and the nonprototype sounds. However, they did not show differential generalization, and thus no *prototype* effect. Evidently, unlike categorical perception, the prototype effect is not based on a perceptual process that is common to monkey and man (Kuhl in press).

Cross-Modal Speech Perception
Thus far I have limited the discussion of infants' perception of speech to auditory events. We typically think of speech as an exclusively auditory phenomenon. Now I extend the discussion to the detection of cross-modal equivalence for speech, wherein categorization abilities go beyond those involving auditory perception.

Recent studies on adults completed in our lab (Green and Kuhl 1989; Green and Kuhl 1991, Grant et al. 1985) and others (McGurk and MacDonald 1976; Massaro 1987; Massaro and Cohen 1983; Green and Miller 1985; Summerfield 1979) show that the perception of speech is strongly influenced by information gleaned from watching the face of a talker. This raises profound problems for a theory of speech perception because it means that visual information, such as watching a talker's lips come together to produce the consonant /b/, is somehow equated in perception to acoustic information that auditorially signals the consonant /b/. (See Kuhl and Meltzoff 1988 for discussion). One important question about such complex cross-modal equivalences is how information as different as the sight of a person producing speech and the auditory speech event that is the result of production come to be related. To answer this, we decided to study the development of the ability to equate auditory and visual speech information.

We designed an experiment to pose a lip-reading problem to infants. We asked whether infants could relate the sight of a person producing a speech sound to the auditory concomitant of that event (Kuhl and Meltzoff 1982). Infants were shown two filmed faces, side by side, of a woman articulating two different vowel sounds. One face displayed productions of the vowel /a/, the other of the vowel /i/. While the infants were viewing the two faces, a single sound, either /a/ or /i/, was presented from a loudspeaker located midway between the two facial images. This eliminated any spatial cues as to which of the two faces produced the sound. The two facial images articulating the sounds moved in perfect synchrony with one another; the lips opened and closed at the exact same time, thus eliminating any temporal cues. The only way an infant could solve the problem was by recognizing a correspondence between the sound and the mouth shape that normally caused that sound. In other words, infants had to perceive a cross-modal match between the auditory and visual representations of speech.

Thirty-two infants ranging in age from 18 to 20 weeks were tested. They were placed in an infant seat facing a three-sided cubicle (figure 5.9). The experiment had two phases, a familiarization phase and a test phase. During familiarization infants saw each of the two faces for ten seconds in the absence of sound. Following this phase both faces were presented side by side, and the sound was turned on. Infants were video- and audio-recorded. An observer who was uninformed about the stimulus conditions scored the videotaped infants' visual fixations to the right or left stimulus.

The hypothesis was that infants would prefer to look at the face that matched the sound. The results confirmed this prediction; infants looked longer at the face that matched the vowel they heard. Infants presented with the auditory /a/ looked longer at the face articulating /a/. Those who heard /i/ looked longer at the face articulating /i/. The effect was strong—of the total looking time, 73 percent was spent on the matched face ($p < .001$) and 24 of the 32 infants demonstrated the effect ($p < .01$). There were no other significant

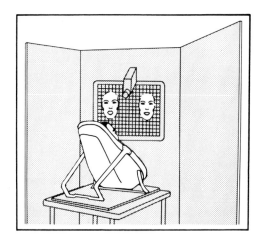

Figure 5.9
Infants' cross-modal speech-perception abilities are tested by presenting them with two facial images, one articulating the vowel /a/ and the other the vowel /i/. One or the other of the two sounds is presented from a loudspeaker midway between the two facial images. The results show that infants look longer at the face that matches the speech sound they heard. (From Kuhl and Meltzoff 1982).

effects—no preference for the face located on the infant's right as opposed to the infant's left side or for the /a/ face as opposed to the /i/ face. There was no significant difference in the strength of the effect when the matching stimulus was located on the infant's right as opposed to the infant's left. (See Kuhl and Meltzoff 1984a for full details.)

We then replicated the findings with 32 additional infants and a new research team (Kuhl and Meltzoff 1984b). All other details of the experiment were identical. The results again showed that infants looked longer at the face that matched the sound they heard. Of the total fixation time, infants spent 62.8 percent fixating the matched face (p <.05), and 23 of the 32 infants demonstrated the effect (p <.01). Recently another team of investigators has also replicated this cross-modal matching effect for speech using disyllables such as *mama* versus *lulu* and *baby* versus *zuzi* in a design similar to ours (MacKain et al. 1983).

Next we extended our tests to another vowel pair (/i-u/), thus including the third "point" vowel in the set of vowels tested. The point vowels are maximally distinct, both acoustically and articulatorily, and occur at the three endpoints of the triangle that defines "vowel space" (Peterson and Barney 1952). The test was conducted just as it had been previously, only this time infants watched faces producing the vowels /i/ and /u/ and listened to either /i/ or /u/ vowels. The results showed that the effect could be extended to a new vowel pair. The mean percentage of fixation time to the matched face was 63.8 percent (p <.05), and 21 of the 32 infants looked longer at the matched face (p <.05) (Kuhl and Meltzoff 1984b).

Thus 4-month-olds perceive auditory-visual equivalents for speech. They recognize that /a/ sounds go with wide-open mouths, /i/ sounds with retracted lips, and /u/ sounds with pursed lips. What accounts for infants' cross-modal speech perception abilities? Have infants learned to associate an open mouth with the sound pattern /a/ and retracted lips with /i/ simply by watching talkers speak? Does some other kind of experience play a role in this ability? Our tests are now being conducted on younger infants to examine the learning account; we are specifically interested in whether or not experience in babbling plays a role in the effect (Kuhl and Meltzoff 1984a).

Vocal Imitation
Thus far in discussing the infant's detection of equivalences in speech the focus has been on the perception of speech through different sensory modalities—auditory and visual. I turn now to speech production to examine another aspect of equivalence that infants detect for speech.

As adults we can produce a specific auditory target, such as a vowel, on the first try. It is not a trial-and-error process. Auditory signals are directly related to the motor commands necessary to produce them because adults have rules that dictate the mapping between articulation and audition. This mapping is quite sophisticated. Experiments show that if an adult speaker is suddenly thwarted in the act of producing a given sound by the introduction of a sudden load imposed on his lip or jaw, compensation is essentially immediate (Abbs and Gracco 1984). The adjustment can occur on the very first laryngeal vibration, prior to the time the adult has heard anything. Such rapid motor adjustments suggest a highly sophisticated and flexible set of rules relating articulatory movements to sound.

How do auditory-articulatory mapping rules develop? Evidence suggests that at least one important mechanism for learning them is vocal imitation (Studdert-Kennedy 1986).

From Piaget on, reports have appeared that are highly suggestive of vocal imitation of at least one prosodic aspect of speech—its pitch (Kessen, Levine, and Wendrich 1979; Lieberman 1984; Papousek and Papousek 1981; Piaget 1962); however, all but one of these studies (Kessen, Levine, and Wendrich 1979) involve natural interactions between adults and infants, and as such are subject to methodological problems (Kuhl and Meltzoff 1988). Natural observations of mothers and their infants are usually subject to the question, Who is imitating whom? The Kessen et al. study tested infants in multiple sessions over several months, giving them repeated practice and feedback, so the issue of training is unresolved in the study.

With these issues in mind we sought evidence of vocal imitation in our own experiments on infants' cross-modal perception of speech (Kuhl and Meltzoff 1982, 1988). The cross-modal studies provided a controlled setting in which to study vocal imitation. Recall our experimental set-up. Infants sat in an infant seat facing a three-sided cubicle. They viewed a film of a female talker producing vowel sounds. Half of the infants were presented with one auditory stimulus while the other half were presented with a different auditory stimulus. The stimuli were totally controlled, both visually and auditorially. There were no human interactions with the infant during the test, and thus no chance for spuriously shaping and/or conditioning a response. The room was a soundproof chamber and a studio-quality microphone was suspended above the infant to obtain clear recordings that could be perceptually or instrumentally analyzed. Finally, the stimulus on film being presented to the infant occurred once every three seconds, with an interstimulus interval of about two seconds. This was ideal for encouraging turn taking on the part of the infant. We found that infants in this setting were calm and highly engaged by the face-voice stimuli. They often listened for a while, smiled at the faces, and then started talking back. Our question was, Do infants' speech vocalizations match those they hear?

In our initial report we described data that were highly suggestive of infants' imitation of the prosodic characteristics of the signal (Kuhl and Meltzoff 1982). We observed an infant matching of the pitch contour of the adult model's vowels. Both the adult's and infant's responses are shown in figure 5.10. Instrumental analysis showed that the infant produced an almost perfect match to the adult female's rise-fall pattern of intonation. While the infant has shorter vocal folds and therefore produces a higher fundamental frequency, the pitch pattern of a rapid rise in frequency followed by a more gradual fall in frequency duplicates that of the adult. The two contours were perceptually very similar. The infant's response also matched the adult's in duration. Because vocalizations with this rise-fall pattern and of this long duration are not common in the utterances of 4-month-olds, it was highly suggestive of vocal imitation. But because we had not varied the pitch pattern of the vowel in the experiment, it was not possible to conclude definitively that infants could differentially match the pitch contour of vowels.

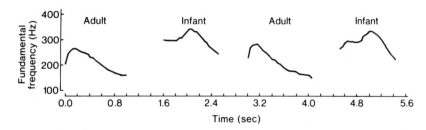

Figure 5.10
Infant vocal imitation of the adult's production of pitch. The infant duplicates the adult's pattern of change in fundamental frequency over time. Both contours show a rise in the fundamental frequency, followed by a gradual fall in the fundamental frequency. The infant's vocal cords are shorter, and thus the infant's rise-fall contour is higher in frequency.

A more rigorous test of young infants' ability to imitate relates to their matching of the phonetic segments of speech. Half of the infants in our experiments had heard /a/ vowels while the other half had heard /i/ vowels. This allowed a good test of the differential imitation of speech sounds. All of the vowel-like vocalizations produced by the infants in the /a-i/ studies were analyzed. Vowel-like sounds were defined on the basis of acoustic and articulatory characteristics typical of vowels. The sounds had to be produced with an open mouth, rather than one that was closed. They had to have a minimum duration of 500 milliseconds. They had to be voiced, that is, vocalized with normal laryngeal vibration, and could not be aspirated or voiceless sounds. They could not be produced on an inhalatory breath. Vocalizations that occurred while the infant's hand was in his or her mouth could not be reliably scored and were excluded. Consonant-like vocalizations were also scored, but they occurred rarely and were always accompanied by vowel-like sounds.

Once identified, the sounds were submitted to analysis. Perceptual scoring was done by having a trained phonetician listen to each infant's productions and judge whether, on the whole, they were more /i/-like or /a/-like. Infants at this age cannot produce perfect /i/ vowels, due to anatomical restrictions. They can, however, produce other high front vowels such as /ɪ/ or /ɜ/. Similarly, a perfect /a/ is rare in the vocalizations of the 4-month-old, but similar central vowels, such as /æ/ and /ʌ/ are producible by infants at this age. Thus the judgment made by the observer was a forced choice concerning whether an infant's vocalizations were more /a/-like or more /i/-like.

If the observers' forced-choice decision predicted whether infants had been exposed to /a/ as opposed to /i/ based on the infant's vocalization, then there is evidence for vocal imitation. The results confirmed this prediction (Kuhl and Meltzoff 1988). Infants' vocalizations were judged to be /a/-like when listening to /a/ and /i/-like when listening to /i/; the judge's forced-choice decisions predicted accurately in 90 percent of the instances the vowel heard by the infant. These results were highly significant ($p < .01$).

We also measured infants' vowels instrumentally. Using distinctive feature theory to guide our instrumental analyses, we measured the first and second formant frequencies of the infants' vowel productions. The results demonstrated that infants' vocal responses to /a/ were significantly more "grave" in feature theory (Jakobson, Fant, and Halle 1969), than their responses to /i/. Similarly, infants' vocal responses to /a/ were significantly more "compact," that is, they had formant frequencies spaced more closely together, than their responses to /i/. Taken together, the two analyses provide evidence that 4-month-old infants are engaged in vocal imitation of the phonetic segments of speech (see Kuhl and Meltzoff 1988 for further details).

Do Animals' Abilities Extend beyond Categorical Perception?

It is now of interest to return to the question of animals' abilities. Human infants' abilities extend well beyond the skills exhibited by categorical perception. Is the same true of animals?

For the four abilities just described—talker normalization, speech prototypes, cross-modal perception, and vocal imitation—we have as yet very little data on animals' abilities. On the topic of talker normalization, there are some data on the perception of categories that include talker variation (Burdick and Miller 1975; Kuhl and Miller 1975, Dooling and Brown 1990), but the data do not include tests on vowel categories that are very similar (as in the case of /a/ versus /ɔ/), so the question of the extent of animals' abilities remains unresolved. We do have data suggesting that the prototype effect exhibited by 6-month-old human infants is not demonstrated by animals (Kuhl in press). This result is intriguing, and we are pursuing it in further studies.

On the ability of animals to detect auditory-visual correspondences for speech, and to vocally imitate speech, we do not as yet have data. We can speculate, however, that these abilities could very well go beyond the capabilities of animals. The ability to detect correspondences between auditorially and visually presented speech may depend on extensive experience in simultaneously watching and listening to spoken language. This is a quite normal occurrence for the human infant, since face-to-face communication between mother and infant begins at birth and flourishes thereafter. But it is not true for a monkey, even for monkeys reared in a laboratory. Alternatively it may be the case that infants' recognition of cross-modal correspondence for speech depends on the infants' recognition that the visual stimulus (the talking face) is "like me," a situation that cannot be duplicated in the monkey. Infants' detection of these correspondences may also require some degree of sound production on the part of the infant, such as that occurring during the early "cooing" stages of speech production.

Finally, the ability to imitate vocally may be beyond the monkey's competence. Monkeys do not imitate sound in the laboratory, nor, apparently, in the wild. Studies of deafened infant macaques, conducted in Japan in the seventies (Green 1975) suggested that infant macaques acquired their vocal repertoires at the same time as normal controls regardless of whether or not they were able to hear the signals that they (or other animals) produced. This is very different from the case in humans where hearing is critical to the development of normal speech production. Thus, we may have uncovered a very important difference between man and monkey.

Discussion

We return now to the question posed at the outset: Are human infants' speech perception abilities unique to the species? Five topics on infants' perception of speech have been reviewed: categorical perception, talker normalization, speech prototypes, the auditory-visual perception of speech, and vocal imitation. The data show that infants display remarkable skill in all of these tasks and that they do so remarkably early in life. Does this mean there is a speech module at work in the baby? The data tempt us to draw this conclusion, but it is probably premature to do so.

Consider first the tests on categorical perception. Here the results are very clear. Infants show the phenomenon, but monkeys and chinchillas do as well. Moreover, categorical perception results are replicable with nonspeech signals (Miller et al. 1976; Pisoni 1977; Pisoni, Carrell, and Gans 1983). It may be, then, that categorical perception for speech reflects a general and basic property of the auditory perceptual system. I have argued that this is no accident (Kuhl 1979b, 1988). In the evolution of speech, sounds were chosen for use as communicative entities—as phonemes—because they were maximally different from an auditory perspective. They fell on opposite sides of these natural psychophysical boundaries. in other words, categorical perception may not be the result of a speech module, rather, speech capitalized on an already existing tendency to carve the world of sound into certain categories (Kuhl and Miller 1978; Kuhl 1988). This would explain why there is so much regularity in the features used universally across languages.

Next, consider the studies that tie production and perception together—auditory-visual speech perception and vocal imitation. Regarding the first, we have shown that infants are capable of linking auditory and visual representations of speech. By 18 weeks they already know what an /a/, and /i/ and /u/ look like on the face of a talker. They can lip-read these sounds (Kuhl and Meltzoff 1982, 1984a, 1984b, 1988). Moreover, as early as 12 weeks of age, there is evidence of vocal imitation (Kuhl and Meltzoff 1988). These abilities are very complex, yet early imitation and cross-modal matching are not unique to the domain of speech. It has been shown that infants imitate soundless gestures such as mouth opening and tongue protrusion very early in life (Meltzoff and Moore 1977, 1983, 1989). In addition, young infants detect cross-modal relations between touch and vision (Bower 1982, Meltzoff and Borton 1979). Evidently, even these extremely sophisticated abilities do not ensure that there is a special speech mechanism at work. They may all be attributable to infants' more general cognitive abilities.

Finally, consider infants' categorization of speech sounds. Our work shows that infants are capable of categorizing speech sounds despite the variability among the members of speech categories (Kuhl 1979a, 1983). The newest results on vowel prototypes suggest that as early as 6 months of age, infants' categorization of speech may be attributable to their recognition of ideal exemplars from the category (Grieser and Kuhl 1989; Kuhl in press). We do not as yet know how prototypes get into the mind of the baby. Finding that out is our current priority. If speech prototypes are built in, then that would be evidence in support of the special mechanism hypothesis. If not, then speech categories, like categories in other domains, may be constructed through experience with exemplars, and this would obviate the need for a special mechanism.

Theoretically there is a pendulum which contrasts the two theoretical views that have been weighed here (Kuhl 1986). One view is that there exists at birth special mechanisms for the perception of speech (Fodor 1983; Liberman and Mattingly 1985). This view received strong support from the results on infants' categorical perception of speech (Eimas et al. 1971). Then when the results on animals were taken into account, the pendulum swung in the opposite direction—toward the view that the infant's behavior can be accounted for by more general auditory perceptual mechanisms (Kuhl 1986, 1987a, 1987b). Now we have the new data on infants discussed here, showing that infants can form categories, recognize prototypes, and detect cross-modal relations for speech. One might be sorely tempted once again to attribute the infants' skills to a special mechanism for speech. But we should probably resist this tendency because there is much evidence to suggest that even these sophisticated abilities are not unique to the domain of speech.

In conclusion, the evidence in hand suggests that human infants may not begin life with a special speech module. Speech procession could well become modularized in adults with increasing experience with the phonological, semantic, and syntactic rules of the language, but it may not begin as a separate entity dedicated to the processing of speech and language. Infants bring to the task of language learning sophisticated abilities that aid them greatly in the language acquisition process. But the sophistication with which they perceive speech signals does not by itself indicate a process that is unique to speech and language. The processing strategies infants employ when acquiring the mother tongue may be rooted in quite general perceptual and cognitive skills.

References

Abbs, J. H., and Gracco, V. L. (1984). Control of complex motor gestures: Orofacial muscle responses to load perturbations of the lip during speech. *Journal of Neurophysiology* 51:705–23.

Anderson, J. A. (1988). Concept formation in neural networks: Implications for evolution of cognitive functions. *Human Evolution* 3:83–100.

Anderson, J. R. (1983). *The Architecture of Cognition.* Cambridge: Harvard University Press.

Aslin, R. N., Pisoni, D. B, Hennessey, B. L., and Perey, A. J. (1981). Discrimination of voice onset time by human infants: New findings and implications for the effects of early experience. *Child Development* 52:1135–45.

Bower, T. G. R. (1982). *Development in infancy.* 2d ed. San Francisco: W. H. Freeman.

Bruner, J. S., Goodnow, J. J., and Austin, G. A. (1956). *A study of thinking.* New York: John Wiley & Sons.

Burdick, C. K., and Miller, J. D. (1975). Speech perception by the chinchilla: Discrimination of sustained [a] and [i]. *Journal of the Acoustical Society of America* 58:415–27.

Chomsky, N. (1980). Rules and representations. *Behavior and Brain Sciences* 3, 1–61.

Dooling, R. J., and Brown, S. D. (1990). Speech perception by Budgerigars (Melopsittacus Undulatis): Spoken vowels. *Perception and Psychophysics* 47, 568–74.

Dooling, R. J., and Hulse, S. H. (1989). *The comparative psychology of audition: Perceiving complex sounds.* Hillsdale, NJ: Lawrence Erlbaum Associates.

Eimas, P. D., Siqueland, E. R., Jusczyk, P., and Vigorito, J. (1971). Speech perception in infants. *Science* 171:303–6.

Fant, G. (1973). *Speech sounds and features.* Cambridge: MIT Press.

Fantz, R. L., and Fagan, J. F., III. (1975). Visual attention to size and number of pattern details by term and preterm infants during the first six months. *Child Development* 46:3–18.

Fernald, A. (1985). Four-month-old infants prefer to listen to motherese. *Infant Behavior and Development* 8:181–95.

Fernald, A., and Kuhl, P. K. (1987). Acoustic determinants of infants' preference for Motherese. *Infant Behavior and Development* 10:279–93.

Fernald, A., and Simon, T. (1984). Expanded intonation contours in mothers' speech to newborns. *Developmental Psychology* 4:104–13.

Fodor, J. A. (1983). *The modularity of mind: An essay on faculty psychology.* Cambridge: MIT Press.

Gardner, B. T., and Gardner, R. A. (1990). Teaching sign language to cross-fostered chimpanzees. *Seminars in Speech and Language* 11:100–118.

Grant, K. W., Ardell, L. H., Kuhl, P. K., and Sparks, D. W. (1985). The contribution of fundamental frequency, amplitude envelope, and voicing duration cues to speechreading in normal-hearing subjects. *Journal of the Acoustical Society of America* 77:671–7.

Green, K. P., and Kuhl, P. K. (1989). The role of visual information in the processing of place and manner features during phonetic perception. *Perception and Psychophysics* 45:34–42.

Green, K. P., and Kuhl, P. K. (1991). Integrality of auditory voicing and visual place information in speech perception. *Journal of Experimental Psychology: Human Perception and Performance.*

Green, K. P., and Miller, J. L. (1985). On the role of visual rate information in phonetic perception. *Perception and Psychophysics* 38:269–76.

Green, S. (1975). Dialects in Japanese monkeys: Vocal learning and cultural transmission of locale-specific vocal behavior *Zeitschrift für Tierpsychologie* 38:304–14.

Grieser, D. L., and Kuhl, P. K. (1988). Maternal speech to infants in a tonal language: Support for universal prosodic features in Motherese. *Developmental Psychology* 24:14–20.

Grieser, D., and Kuhl, P. K. (1989). Categorization of speech by infants: Support for speech-sound prototypes. *Developmental Psychology* 25:577–88.

Kagan, J., Henker, B. A., Hen-Tov, A., Levine, J., and Lewis, M. (1966). Infants' differential reactions to familiar and distorted faces. *Child Development* 37:519–32.

Kessen, W., Levine, J., and Wendrich, K. A. (1979). The imitation of pitch in infants. *Infant Behavior and Development* 2:93–99.

Kuhl, P. K. (1979a). Models and mechanisms in speech perception: Species comparisons provide further contributions. *Brain, Behavior and Evolution* 16:374:408.

Kuhl, P. K. (1979b). Speech perception in early infancy: Perceptual constancy for spectrally dissimilar vowel categories. *Journal of the Acoustical Society of America* 66:1668–79.

Kuhl, P. K. (1983). The perception of auditory equivalence classes for speech in early infancy. *Infant Behavior and Development* 6:263–85.

Kuhl, P. K. (1986). Theoretical contributions of tests on animals to the special-mechanisms debate in speech. *Experimental Biology* 45:233–65.

Kuhl, P. K. (1987a). Perception of speech and sound in early infancy. In *Handbook of infant perception, Vol. 2, From perception to cognition,* ed. P. Salapatek and L. B. Cohen, 275–382. New York: Academic Press.

Kuhl, P. K. (1987b). The special-mechanisms debate in speech: Categorization tests on animals and infants. In *Categorical perception: The groundwork of cognition,* ed. S. Harnad, 355–86. Cambridge: Cambridge University Press.

Kuhl, P. K. (1988). Auditory perception and the evolution of speech. *Human Evolution* 3:19–43.

Kuhl, P. K. (In press). Human adults and human infants exhibit a "prototype effect" for speech sounds: Monkeys do not. *Perception and Psychophysics*.

Kuhl, P. K., Green, K. P., Gordon, J. W., Sanford, D. L., and Fu, C. (1989). Word recognition by humans and machines: Tests on multi-talker, multistyle database. *Journal of Acoustical Society of America* 86:Suppl. 1, S77 (A).

Kuhl, P. K., and Meltzoff, A. N. (1982). The bimodal perception of speech in infancy. *Science* 218:1138–41.

Kuhl, P. K., and Meltzoff, A. N. (1984a). The intermodal representation of speech in infants. *Infant Behavior and Development* 7:361–81.

Kuhl, P. K., and Meltzoff, A. N. (1984b). Infants' recognition of cross-modal correspondence for speech: Is it based on physics or phonetics? *Journal of the Acoustical Society of America* 76:Suppl. 1, S80 (A).

Kuhl, P. K., and Meltzoff, A. N. (1988). Speech as an intermodal object of perception. In *The development of perception: Minnesota symposia on child psychology* ed. A. Yonas, 235–66. Hillsdale, NJ: Lawrence Erlbaum Associates.

Kuhl, P. K., and Miller, J. D. (1975). Speech perception by the chinchilla: Voiced-voiceless distinction in alveolar plosive consonants. *Science* 190:69–72.

Kuhl, P. K., and Miller, J. D. (1978). Speech perception by the chinchilla: Identification functions for synthetic VOT stimuli. *Journal of the Acoustical Society of America* 63:905–17.

Kuhl, P. K., and Padden, D. M. (1982). Enhanced discriminability at the phonetic boundaries for the voicing feature in macaques. *Perception and Psychophysics* 32:542–50.

Kuhl, P. K., and Padden, D. M. (1983). Enhanced discriminability at the phonetic boundaries for the place feature in macaques. *Journal of the Acoustical Society of America* 73:1003–10.

Lasky, R. E., Syrdal-Lasky, A., and Klein, R. E. (1975). VOT discrimination by four to six and a half month old infants from Spanish environments. *Journal of Experimental Child Psychology* 20:215–25.

Liberman, A. M., Cooper, F. S., Shankweiler, D. P., and Studdert-Kennedy, M. (1967). Perception of the speech code. *Psychological Review* 74:431–61.

Liberman, A. M. and Mattingly, I. (1985). The motor theory of speech perception revised. *Cognition* 21:1–36.

Liberman, A. M., Mattingly I., and Turvey, M. T. (1972). Language codes and memory codes. In *Coding processes in human memory*, ed. A. W. Melton, & E. Martin. New York: John Wiley & Sons.

Lieberman, P. (1984). *The biology and evolution of language*. Cambridge: Harvard University Press.

Lieberman, P. (In press). *Speech, thought and selfless behavior*. Cambridge: Harvard University Press.

McGurk, H., and MacDonald, J. (1976). Hearing lips and seeing voices. *Nature* 264:746–48.

MacKain, K.; Studdert-Kennedy, M.; Spieker, S.; and Stern, D. (1983). Infant intermodal speech perception is a left-hemisphere function. *Science* 219:1347–49.

Massaro, D. W. (1987). *Speech perception by ear and eye: A paradigm for psychological inquiry*. Hillsdale, NJ: Lawrence Erlbaum Associates.

Massaro, D. W., and Cohen, M. M. (1983). Evaluation and integration of visual and auditory information in speech perception. *Journal of Experimental Psychology: Human Perception and Performance* 9:753–71.

Medin, D. L., and Barsalou, L. W. (1987). Categorization processes and categorical perception. In *Categorical perception: The ground work of cognition*, ed. S. Harnad, 455–490. Cambridge: Cambridge University Press.

Meltzoff, A. N. (1988). Imitation, objects, tools and the rudiments of language. *Human Evolution* 3:45–64.

Meltzoff, A. N., and Borton, R. W. (1979). Intermodal matching by human neonates. *Nature* 282:403–4.

Meltzoff, A. N., and Moore, M. K. (1977). Imitation of facial and manual gestures by human neonates. *Science* 198:75–78.

Meltzoff, A. N., and Moore, M. K. (1983). Newborn infants imitate adult facial gestures. *Child Development* 54:702–9.

Meltzoff, A. N., and Moore, M. K. (1989). Imitation in newborn infants: Exploring the range of gestures imitated and the underlying mechanisms. *Developmental Psychology* 25:954–62.

Miller, J. D., Wier, C. C., Pastore, R. E., Kelly, W. J., and Dooling R. J. (1976). Discrimination and labeling of noise-buzz sequences with varying noise-lead times: An example of categorical perception. *Journal of the Acoustical Society of America* 60:410–17.

Miller, J. L. (1977). Properties of feature detectors for VOT: The voiceless channel of analysis. *Journal of the Acoustical Society of America* 62:641–48.

Miller, J. L., and Volaitis, L. E. (1989). Effect of speaking rate on the perceptual structure of a phonetic category. *Perception and Psychophysics* 46:505–12.

Miyawaki, K., Strange, W., Verbrugge, R., Liberman, A. M., Jenkins, J. J., and Fujimura, O. (1975). An effect of linguistic experience: The discrimination of [r] and [l] by native speakers of Japanese and English. *Perception and Psychophysics* 18:331–40.

Mullennix, J. W., and Pisoni, D. B. (1990). Stimulus variability and processing dependencies in speech perception. *Perception and Psychophysics* 47:379–90.

Mullennix, J. W., Pisoni, D. B., and Martin, C. S. (1989). Some effects of talker variability on spoken word recognition. *Journal of the Acoustical Society of America* 85:365–78.

Papousek, H., and Papousek, M. (1981). Musical elements in the infant's vocalization: Their significance for communication, cognition, and creativity. In *Advances in infancy research*, ed. L. P. Lipsitt and C. K. Rovee-Collier, 164–224. Norwood, NJ: Ablex.

Peterson, G. E., and Barney, H. L. (1952). Control methods used in a study of the vowels. *Journal of the Acoustical Society of America* 24:175–84.

Piaget, J. (1962). *Play, dreams, and imitation in childhood*. New York: Norton.

Pisoni, D. B. (1977). Identification and discrimination of the relative onset time of two component tones: Implications for voicing perception in stops. *Journal of the Acoustical Society of America* 61:1352–61.

Pisoni, D. B., Carrell, T. D., and Gans, S. J. (1983). Perception of the duration of rapid spectrum changes in speech and nonspeech signals. *Perception and Psychophysics* 34:314–22.

Rosch, E. (1975). Cognitive reference points. *Cognitive Psychology* 7:532–47.

Rumelhart, D. E., McClelland, J. L., and the PDP Research Group. (1986). *Parallel distributed processing: Exploration in the microstructures of cognition*. Cambridge: MIT Press.

Samuel, A. G. (1982). Phonetic prototypes. *Perception and Psychophysics* 31:307–14.

Stevens, K. N. (1972). The quantal nature of speech: Evidence from articulatory-acoustic data. In *Human communication: A unified view*, ed. J. E. E. David and P. D. Denes, 51–66. New York: McGraw-Hill.

Stevens, K. N. (1981). Constraints imposed by the auditory system on the properties used to classify speech sounds: Evidence from phonology, acoustics, and psychoacoustics. In *Advances in psychology: The cognitive representation of speech,* ed. T. Myers, J. Laver, and J. Anderson. Amsterdam: North-Holland.

Stevens, S. S., Volkman, J., and Newman, E. B. (1937). A scale for the measurement of the psychological magnitude pitch. *Journal of the Acoustical Society of America* 8:185–90.

Streeter, L. A. (1976). Language perception of 2-month-old infants shows effects of both innate mechanisms and experience. *Nature* 259:39–41.

Studdert-Kennedy, M. (1986). Development of the speech perceptuomotor system. In *Precursors of early speech,* ed. B. Lindblom and R. Zetterström, 205–18. New York: Stockton Press.

Summerfield, Q. (1979). Use of visual information for phonetic perception. *Phonetica* 36:314–31.

Chapter 6

The Instinct for Vocal Learning: Songbirds

Peter Marler

Most of us tend to think of learning and instinct as irreconcilable opposites. Whether human or animal, behavior is construed as either learned or instinctive, but it cannot be both. According to this view animals display instincts, but our behavior is learned. We are presumed to exemplify what organisms can accomplish by the emancipation of behavior from instinctive control.

This antithesis is based on a logical fallacy. Even when we contemplate the most extreme case of purely arbitrary, culturally transmitted behavior, such as songbird dialects (Baker and Cunningham 1985) or our own patterns of speech, it is obvious on reflection that such behavior must in some sense be the result of an instinct at work. Without the bones and muscles, nerves and patterns of brain activity, and the very special capacity of nervous systems to forego existing predispositions and to reshape their activities as a result of experience, the cultural transmission of behavior would be inconceivable.

Similarly, the traditional view of instincts as fixed and immutable manifestations of purely genetic predispositions is also at fault. All behavior, whether it is viewed as instinctive or learned, develops out of an interaction between the genetic endowment of the embryo and the environment within which development takes place. Ontogenetic programs do differ in the degree to which they are open to influence by the developmental environment, however. Some are relatively closed and designed to resist or counteract displacements from a particular, specified ontogenetic trajectory. Others are genetically designed to be more open and malleable in the face of experience. It is toward this end of the closed-open continuum that culturally transmitted behavior falls. If we compare the behavior of individuals with

Research was conducted in collaboration with Susan Peters and supported by grant number MH14651. Esther Arruza prepared the figures, and Sondra O'Rourke typed the manuscript. I thank Judith and Cathy Marler and Eileen McCue for rearing the birds. I am indebted to Susan Peters, Stephen Nowicki, and Robert Dooling for discussion and criticism of the manuscript, and to the New York Botanical Garden Institute of Ecosystem Studies at the Mary Flagler Cary Arboretum for access to study areas.

different experiential histories, the variations we see have a greater environmental component in behavioral systems at the open end of the continuum and more of a genetic component at the closed end; but in no case can development take place without crucial contributions from both genetics and environment. Both participate in every ontogenetic equation.

Thus to speak of *instincts to learn* is not as paradoxical as it at first appears (Gould and Marler 1984). I am inclined to favor the term, if only for didactic purposes, to draw attention to the predispositions that animals bring to learning situations, arising out of their past history. I find this particular turn of phrase useful because it explicitly acknowledges an often overlooked reality of behavioral development, namely, the inescapable role of genetic contributions. The appropriate question to pose is thus not, Do instincts to learn exist? but rather, What is their nature, and by what mechanisms do they operate? Concepts from classical ethology are instructive in searching for answers to questions such as these (Lorenz 1965; Tinbergen 1951).

Three concepts from ethology are especially germane. One is the notion of *sensitive periods*, defined as phases of development during which organisms possess both special sensitivity to particular patterns of environmental stimulation and an unusual potential for behavioral lability. The complementary ethological concepts of *releasers (sign stimuli)* and *innate release mechanisms* are also useful in trying to understand the interplay of genetic and environmental factors in behavioral development. They are invoked to explain the remarkable fact that many organisms, especially during infancy, are attuned to be especially responsive to certain key stimuli, responding to them as they interact with their companions and with their physical environments and being changed themselves in the process. This attunement to specific stimuli implies the possession of neural mechanisms within the infant brain that inculcate sensitivity to certain kinds of stimulation and favor certain modes of responsiveness to them.

Instincts vary in their specificity. The functions of some are generalized, tending to facilitate, for example, broadly positive reactions to certain kinds of stimuli and repugnance to others. Other instincts engender more specific predispositions, linking certain stimuli with particular sets of behaviors or limiting the potential for development plasticity to certain behavioral domains. We cannot predict the effects of a particular experience on the developing behavior of a young organism until we understand the properties and predispositions of the particular set of neural subsystems within the brain that are assigned to the processing of information about such experiences.

One service that the theories of classical ethology can provide is to focus attention on behavioral systems that lend themselves to experimentation and illustrate the interplay of genetic and environmental factors in development with particular clarity. It has become evident in recent years that such concepts as sign stimuli and innate release mechanisms have richer and more interesting functions than simply serving as design features for animals as automata. They are more appropriately viewed as serving to facilitate and guide the development of behavior toward varying degrees of sensitivity and responsiveness to environmental change. In particular such mechanisms facilitate and guide learning processes as components in what I have come to view, informally, as instincts to learn.

My own research on song learning in birds illustrates that even with behavior that is, without any equivocation, learned, each species of bird brings its own particular set of distinctive predispositions to the task of learning to sing (Marler 1984). The invocation of instincts to learn follows naturally, once the crucial point is taken that instincts are not immutable. Although they are often relatively resistant to environmental change, instincts do not lack developmental plasticity and are themselves in some degree modifiable as a result of experience. The degree of modifiability is sometimes minor and sometimes so great that it becomes hard to establish the role of the instinct that is at work.

Preferences in Song Learning

We are prone to thinking of ourselves as capable of learning virtually anything, given sufficient time and motivation. Therefore, we often overlook the overwhelming tendency for most of us to approach learning problems in a particular way. How else could there be sufficient commonalities in language for us to use it to communicate with one another? Birds are no exception.

If we present young birds of different species with a wide array of songs or tutors to learn from, do they all treat them the same, or are they more discriminating, perhaps favoring songs of their own kind? The strategy I have adopted in my studies of song learning in birds is to bring young males of two species into the laboratory and rear them under identical conditions. In this way we give them the opportunity to reveal any particular predispositions they may possess that vary from species to species. Are there instincts to learn song that are in any way distinct in, say, two different species of sparrows?

Despite the close genetic relationship of swamp and song sparrows, their songs are very different (figure 6.1). One is simple, the

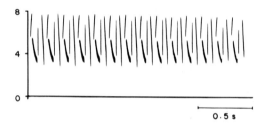

0·5 s

Figure 6.1
Sound spectrograms of a song sparrow song and a swamp sparrow song. The frequency (vertical) scale is marked in kilohertz. A half-second marker is indicated on the time scale (horizontal). Songs of the two species differ not only in acoustic structure but also in repertoire size. A male swamp sparrow has about three different song types, a male song sparrow ten or twelve.

other more complex. Their songs differ in overall syntax and also in phonology, in ways that we can hear—a bird watcher can distinguish them instantly on hearing a single song. They also differ in other respects, such as the size of their individual song repertoires. A male swamp sparrow has two or three song types, and a song sparrow three or four times as many.

How do males of these two species proceed to learn their songs if we bring them into the laboratory as nestlings, raise them by hand to limit their opportunity to hear song, and then expose them, as fledglings, to tape recordings of song? We know that they are capable of copying other species' songs, especially if we give them no chance to hear songs of their own species (figure 6.2). How do they behave if we give them a choice by providing equal numbers of natural swamp sparrow and song sparrow songs (Marler and Peters 1988b, 1989)? When we analyze the songs that they produce some months later, it is clear that each bird prefers to learn songs of its own species (conspecific songs) rather than those of the other species (heterospecific songs). As we inspect the results of this experiment, (see figure 6.3) we also note that the conspecific preference in learning from tape recordings is notably stronger in swamp sparrows than in song sparrows. This is true both of birds taken into the laboratory as nestlings, with a chance perhaps to hear song for a few days around the time of hatching, and of birds raised from the egg by hand, with no previous opportunity to hear the song of their species even prior to hatching.

Neither bird is known to copy the other species in nature. It may be that the opportunity for social interaction with live tutors known to exert an influence on learning preferences in some songbirds (see Baptista and Petrinovich 1984) is more important in song sparrows than in swamp sparrows (Marler and Peters 1988a), indicating another avenue by which experience can exert an influence on song learning.

On what acoustic features are preferences of newly hatched songbirds based? The answer depends on the species. We created computer-synthesized songs in which different acoustic features had been independently varied and presented them for song learning (Marler and Peters 1988b, 1989). The results reveal that the conspecific preference of male swamp sparrows is based not on syntactical features of the song but on the phonology of the syllables. Male swamp sparrows presented with simplified songs consisting either of swamp sparrow syllables or of song sparrow syllables unerringly favored those with conspecific syllables, regardless of the temporal pattern in which they were presented. When swamp sparrows reproduced them in song, the syllables were recast in the normal swamp sparrow syntax,

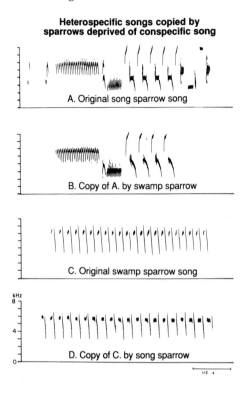

**Heterospecific songs copied by
sparrows deprived of conspecific song**

A. Original song sparrow song

B. Copy of A. by swamp sparrow

C. Original swamp sparrow song

D. Copy of C. by song sparrow

Figure 6.2
Birds are capable of learning and producing songs of other species from tape recordings, especially if they have no opportunity to hear songs of their own species, as
shown here for a swamp sparrow and a song sparrow raised in the laboratory.

whether or not this pattern was present in the songs they heard (figure 6.4). In choosing models for learning, the syllable is the primary
focus of interest for a swamp sparrow.

In contrast song sparrows, with their more complex songs, based
their learning preferences not only on syllabic structure but also on
tempo and on a number of syntactical features, including the number
of segments into which the song was divided and the internal structure of those segments, such as whether syllables were trilled or un-
repeated. Thus song sparrows are guided by cues different from those
of swamp sparrows, who do not refer to any of these syntactical features when they chose models for song learning. Presented with the
very same set of computer-synthesized songs when they are learning
to sing, members of the two species thus behave very differently.

The evidence indicates that young birds respond to specifically dis-

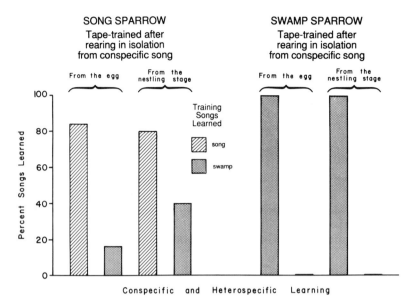

Figure 6.3
Learning preferences of male song and swamp sparrows either raised in the laboratory from the egg or exposed to song in nature during the nestling phase and then brought into the laboratory. Birds were given a choice of tape recordings to learn—some of their own species' songs and some of the other species'. The results show that both have a preference for learning songs of their own species, but the preference is stronger in swamp sparrows than in song sparrows. Song experience during the nestling stage evidently has no effect on learning preferences.

tinctive song features, even at the very beginning of the process of learning to sing. Using heart rate deceleration as an index, Dooling and Searcy (1980) found that young sparrows respond more to conspecific than to heterospecific song. As with behavioral tests, swamp sparrows were more selective than song sparrows by this measure also. Such selective responsiveness to conspecific signals—thought in the early days of ethology to be a special feature of instinctive behavior—is used in this case as the basis for a learning process. Having focused attention on the particular set of exemplars that satisfy certain preordained criteria, the birds proceed to learn these songs, often in great detail, encompassing not only general characteristics of the species song but also the local dialect represented (if the species possesses song dialects).

In the swamp sparrow song dialects are defined by the pattern of notes within a syllable (Marler and Pickert 1984; Balaban 1988a, 1988b, 1988c). Experiments on adult birds reveal that both males and females

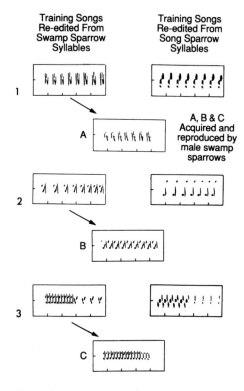

Figure 6.4
Examples of three pairs of synthetic songs presented for young male swamp sparrows to learn, together with the three imitations based on them. Only swamp sparrow syllables were acquired, irrespective of the syntax of the synthetic song. **A** is a relatively faithful rendition of the model. In **B** and **C** syllables of the model are rendered accurately, but the syntax is modified to normal swamp sparrow pattern.

acquire responsiveness to these learned dialects. Thus birds go far beyond the dictates of any simple, unmodifiable lock-and-key mechanism, once the underlying physiological mechanisms have served to set the framework within which learning can proceed.

A further important point is that when birds learn songs, they are not completely bound to observe these preferences. If conspecific songs are withheld or if a bird is caged with an intensely reactive heterospecific singing tutor, it can be persuaded to learn nonpreferred songs (Baptista and Petrinovich 1984). Heterospecific songs are within a bird's vocal compass, even though they would be eschewed in the normal course of events, assuming that circumstances allow preferences to be displayed. Thus learning preferences are not mandatory but establish a certain probabilistic trajectory to the ontogenetic process. Song learning serves well to illustrate one of the ways in which instincts to learn operate, namely, by exploiting the predictability of certain aspects of the environment—in this case, the probability that conspecific tutors will both be available and likely to be more reactive companions than members of other species.

Alien songs may be rendered more acceptable by the simple step of embedding within them notes of the bird's own species (figure 6.5). Thus the sign stimuli present in conspecific songs operate not only as behavioral triggers but also as cues for learning, constituting what we might think of as *enabling signals*. These signals are stimuli whose presence increases the probability of learning other associated stimuli that might otherwise be neglected. This function is served by many sign stimuli, and it may be their primary function, rather than the simple triggering of instinctive behavior, as was thought in the early days of ethology.

Auditory Templates for Song

Regardless of what song patterns they have experienced previously, young sparrows are able to generate several aspects of the syntax of their species song. This potential is most clearly displayed by birds raised in isolation from all song (Marler and Sherman 1985). There are many abnormalities in the sound patterns they produce, but both song and swamp sparrows are nevertheless capable of producing features of conspecific syntax (figure 6.6). The song syntax of a male swamp sparrow is in fact somewhat resistant to change by experience, although not completely so (Marler and Peters 1980). We have noted that males of this species copy syllables more readily than they copy whole songs. This is not the case with song sparrows. When a male song sparrow learns a song of its own species, it sometimes imitates

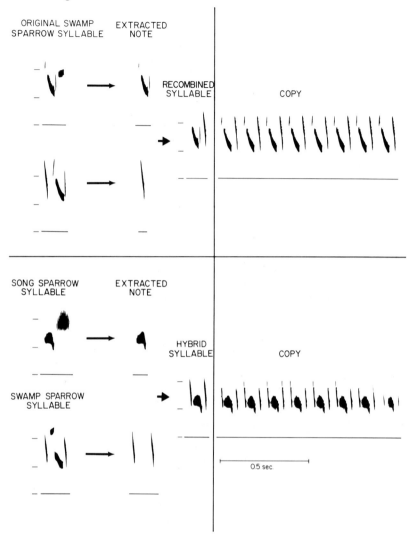

Figure 6.5
Male swamp sparrows normally reject song sparrow notes as learning stimuli but will accept them if they are embedded in swamp sparrow syllables. The bottom panel shows the creation of such a hybrid syllable and its imitation by a male swamp sparrow on the right. The top panel illustrates the control procedure, in which only swamp sparrow notes are transposed and copied.

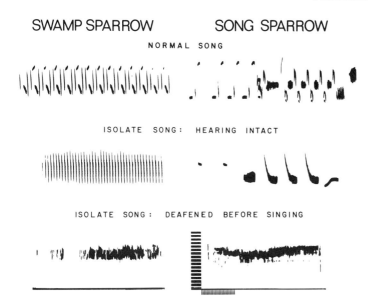

Figure 6.6
Sound spectrograms illustrating typical songs of swamp and song sparrows produced under three conditions. Row 1: Sparrows with normal learning in the wild. Row 2: Sparrows reared in isolation with hearing intact. Row 3: Deaf sparrows reared in isolation. (Kay Digital Sonagraph Model 7800, 8 kHz analysis range, 300-Hz analysis band width. Frequency markers are 1-kHz intervals, time marker is 0.5 seconds.)

the entire syntax, idiosyncratic though that song may be. Clearly the prior possession of responsiveness to syntax does not preclude developmental plasticity in responsiveness to snytax. Again we are reminded that predispositions to react to species-specific stimulus characteristics do not necessarily imply immutability of that responsiveness. Evidently there are predispositions for mutability as such, along certain specified structural dimensions of song.

Where should we look in the brain for the physiological mechanisms that underlie the ability to respond to species-specific song characteristics? Some insight is gained by studying the singing behavior of deaf birds (figure 6.6). Hearing is important not only for a bird to respond to the songs of others but also to permit it to hear its own voice so that the brain can monitor singing behavior. The songs that a deaf male sparrow develops are highly abnormal (Konishi 1965; Marler and Sherman 1983). They vary greatly in structure, which is almost amorphous, but a few basic species features can still be discerned. This degraded form of song, which is meaningless to other sparrows (Searcy and Marler 1987), results if a male becomes deaf either before any experience of song or after song stimulation but before the development of its own singing. There seems to be no internal brain circuitry that makes memorized songs directly available to guide motor development. To transform a memorized song into a produced song, the bird must be able to hear its own voice.

The discovery by Konishi (1965) leads to the concept of song-learning templates in the bird brain providing a bridge between early learning preferences and later song production and mediating in the assimilation of the effects of relevant intervening experiences. The concept of auditory templates provides one simple model of the kind of brain mechanism involved in instincts to learn (Marler 1976). Although it originates from studies of song learning in birds, this model is applicable to other behaviors that are dependent on sensory feedback from motor activity to guide development. Feedback is referred to a template system in the brain possessing specifications that both guide the developmental process and are supplemented, modified, or overridden by experiences that take place at certain times and in particular, specified circumstances.

Plans for Motor Development

In most birds the imitation of others plays no role in the process of normal song development. This is the case with flycatchers, for example. When such a bird begins to sing, the first efforts are clearly identifiable as immature versions of what will ultimately become the normal, crystallized song (Kroodsma 1984). These early efforts may be noisy and fragmented, but the maturational progression is clear and predictable.

In birds that learn their songs from others such as the oscine songbirds, there is an equally predictable developmental progression that is quite different (Marler and Peters 1982b). They begin with subsong, which then metamorphoses into plastic song, and eventually becomes the mature song of the species (figure 6.7). The progression may be rapid or protracted, but the sequence through stages that are quite different in structure seems to recur in all birds that must learn to sing.

The phenomenon of subsong is of special interest, reminding us as it does of the babbling phase of speech development. Its structure, which is quite different from that of mature song, is amorphous and noisy, but these characteristics disappear as it is transformed into the orderly structure, first of plastic song, and then of the formalized morphology of crystallized song. There are many mysteries about the functional significance of subsong. It is believed to be critical for de-

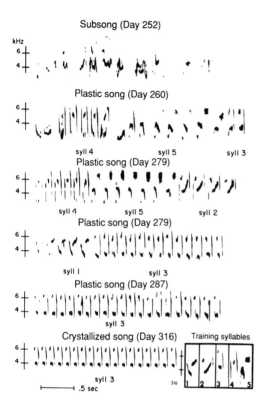

Figure 6.7

A sampling of stages of song development in a male swamp sparrow from 252 to 316 days of age, showing the transitions from subsong through plastic song to full, crystallized song. This bird crystallized two themes, one of which, using syllable 3, is illustrated. Syllables of some of the training songs to which the male was exposed in youth are shown at the bottom right. The tendency for overproduction during plastic song can be clearly seen.

veloping the motor skills of singing and also for perfecting the ability
to guide the voice by the ear. This vocal-auditory link appears to be a
prerequisite for vocal imitation but is irrelevant for song development
in song species in which imitation plays no role.

Only in the second stage, plastic song, are there any obvious signs
of mature song structure. As plastic song progresses, we begin to see
signs of rehearsal of previously memorized songs. The patterns sta-
bilize gradually until crystallization occurs. Plastic song has interesting characteristics, some of which suggest that it can be viewed as a
kind of vocal play. Song material is produced in abundance during
plastic song, with many themes that are subsequently discarded as
crystallization takes place (Marler and Peters 1982a). If we sum data
on the numbers of songs present in an individual male swamp sparrow's repertoire during this transition from plastic to crystallized song,
we find that whereas a typical crystallized repertoire is two or three
song types, there may be five times as many song themes in plastic
song (figure 6.8). Some are invented themes, but many of these ov-
erproduced songs are imitations of themes heard earlier in life. Evidently more is memorized by the young bird than is manifest in the
final products of motor development. One wonders whether memory

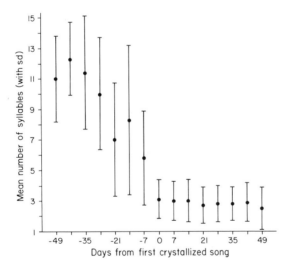

Figure 6.8
A plot of the number of syllables that types of individual male swamp sparrows produced at different stages of song development, arranged around day 0 as the time
when song became crystallized. At this stage males produce a normal song repertoire
of two or three song types. There is extensive overproduction of song types in earlier
stages of song development.

traces of unused songs are discarded or perhaps used for other purposes later in life, such as distinguishing neighbors from strangers, or guilding decisions about where to establish a territory and whom to mate with.

Steps in Learning to Sing: Sensitive Periods

There is an underlying pattern in the sequence of steps required for a bird to learn to sing. First, in the acquisition phase songs heard are subjected to auditory processing and some are committed to memory. These memorized songs are then stored for a period of time that varies from species to species, until the bird begins retrieving some songs from memory. Subsong may occur prior to this stage, but the onset of active rehearsal of previously memorized songs is the sign that plastic song has begun. Themes are rehearsed and stabilized, and then crystallization occurs. In swamp sparrows this is quite a sudden event, involving some dramatic changes in the organization of singing behavior.

One aspect of instincts to learn is the occurrence of phases of life in which the organism is especially predisposed to learn certain things. There are many such sensitive periods for learning during life, and those for song acquisition are sometimes especially well defined. They may be brief or so extended that it can be difficult to separate one particular sensitive period from another.

There are striking differences between species in the timing of sensitive periods (Marler 1987; Marler and Peters 1987, 1988a). In some, song acquisition is age dependent and restricted to a very short period early in life. In others the ability to acquire new songs may persist throughout life. Even close relatives such as sparrows and canaries differ in the duration and timing of sensitive periods. Experiments must be conducted to specify exactly when they occur.

By playing a changing medley of tape-recorded songs to male sparrows in the laboratory throughout their first year of life and recording and analyzing the songs produced, we have been able to extrapolate when acquisition occurred, in this way reconstructing the timing of the sensitive period. In male swamp sparrows song acquisition begins at about 20 days after hatching, peaks at about 50 days of age, and then declines, to end at about 100 days, before the onset of plastic song. In male song sparrows the sensitive period for song acquisition is more compressed (figure 6.9). Such differences between species offer us ideal opportunities to study the neural and hormonal changes responsible for timing of these sensitive learning periods.

As with other aspects of instincts to learn, these sensitive periods

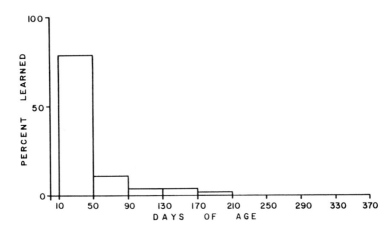

Figure 6.9
The sensitive period for song acquisition in male song sparrows peaks between 10 and 50 days of age. These results were obtained by training song sparrows with constantly changing programs of tape-recorded songs and then inferring the age at which acquisition occurred from analyses of songs produced later in life.

are not fixed traits. There are degrees of lability, depending upon such factors as the strength of song stimulation and the bird's hormonal state, varying with the season. Young of some species are hatched so late that the singing season has already closed for that year. In such cases termination of the sensitive period may be delayed until the following spring. Depriving a bird of access to songs of its own species can also delay closure of the sensitive period. The fact that each species has a distinctive program for acquiring song does not mean that the potential for behavioral flexibility is sacrificed. Rather a distinctive species-specified context is established, within which individual experience can reshape behavior in particular ways.

Species Differences in Inventiveness and Creativity

Some birds imitate learned models closely, and local dialects are widespread in such species. Even in these cases, however, a degree of individuality in song structure is virtually universal. In every songbird studied this individuality provides an adequate basis for birds to discriminate among neighbors and to tell neighbors from strangers.

While all songbirds display some degree of inventiveness in the process of developing song, species differ greatly in the extent to which this creative potential is exercised and in the form it takes. Consider, for example, the recasting or reediting of components of learned songs into new sequences. This is one widespread means for generating novelty and for producing the very large individual repertories that some birds possess, consisting of hundreds of different song types. In the process of developing song, such species often break learned themes down into phrases or syllables and then reorder them in different sequences that become stable themes.

The components for rearrangement may be drawn from different parts of the same song or from different songs (figure 6.10), and even from themes acquired at different times, as we have demonstrated in the song sparrow. The rules for this process—in which acquired songs are parsed down into components and then built into new songs by recombining the components in various ways—differ from species to species. There is also species variation in the faithfulness with which a bird adheres to the structure of a given learned model. Some, like the sparrows, are relatively conservative. They recast syllables often, but they adhere to the basic syllabic structure of a model. Other species, such as the red-winged blackbird, are compulsive improvisers.

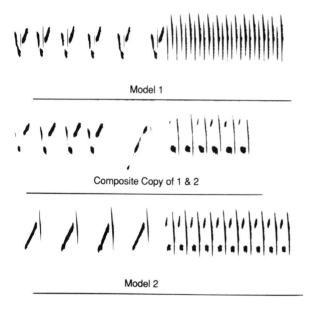

Figure 6.10
Song sparrows often create new themes by breaking learned songs down into their component syllables and recombining them in various ways. Illustrated here is the song of a laboratory-reared song sparrow exposed to an array of synthetic songs. It learned two of these (1 and 2) and recombined parts of them, as illustrated, to create a crude approximation of normal song sparrow song syntax.

Like a jazz musician, they subject a given learned theme to continuous experimentation during development, until the original theme is barely recognizable. This drive to indulge in compulsive improvisation is one reason we shifted attention in our song learning studies from blackbirds to sparrows.

Such species differences in creative aspects of song development suggest that we can conceive of instincts for inventiveness. The ubiquitousness of individuality in bird song implies that vocal development is inherently a creative process. The array of forms that inventiveness can take is still governed, however, by sets of rules that differ from species to species.

The Implication of Species Differences in Song Learning

The studies I have reviewed show that each bird species has its own distinctive set of brain mechanisms for constraining or encouraging improvisation, imposing and guiding learning preferences of varying degree, directing patterns of motor development, and establishing times when the sensitivity for acquiring new information from the environment is especially acute.

Bird songs are learned, and yet species-specific biases and predispositions intrude at every turn of the learning process, offering priceless opportunities for the developmental biologist to pinpoint the ways in which changes in gene activity, hormonal production, and growth and plasticity of the nervous system can affect the process of learning a new behavior.

The proverbial bird brain has already yielded many secrets about the neurobiology of vocal plasticity. Yet there is a sense in which we have hardly begun to exploit the potential of *comparative* studies. In the search for new insights into the physiological bases of instincts to learn, the approaches pioneered by ethologists such as Konrad Lorenz and Niko Tinbergen may be a special source of inspiration and guidance.

References

Baker, M. C., and Cunningham. M. A. (1985). The biology of birdsong dialects. *Behav. and Brain Sci.* 8:85–133.

Balaban, E. (1988a). Cultural and genetic variation in swamp sparrows (*Melospiza georgiana*): I. Song variation, genetic variation, and their relationship. *Behavior* 105:250–91.

Balaban, E. (1988b). Cultural and genetic variation in swamp sparrows (*Melospiza georgiana*): II. Behavioral significance of geographic song variants. *Behavior* 105:292–322.

Balaban, E. (1988c). Bird song syntax: Learned intraspecific variation is meaningful. *Proc. Natl. Acad. Sci.* 85:3657–60.

Baptista, L. F., and Petrinovich, L. (1984). Social interaction, the sensitive phases and the song template hypothesis in the white-crowned sparrow. *Anim. Behav.* 32:172–81.

Dooling, R. J., and Searcy, M. H. (1980). Early perceptual selectivity in the swamp sparrow. *Anim. Behav.* 32:172–81.

Gould, J. L., and Marler, P. (1984). Ethology and the natural history of learning. In *The biology of learning*, ed. P. Marler and H. S. Terrace, New York: Springer-Verlag.

Konishi, M. (1965). The role of auditory feedback in the control of vocalization in the white-crowned sparrow. *Zeitschrift fur Tierpsychologie* 22:770–83.

Kroodsma, D. E. (1984). Songs of the alder flycatcher *(Empidonax alnorum)* and willow flycatcher *(Empidonax traillii)* are innate. *Auk* 101:13–24.

Lorenz, K. S. (1965) *Evolution and Modification of Behavior*. Chicago: Chicago University Press.

Marler, P. (1976). Sensory templates in the species-specific behavior. In. *Simpler networks and behavior*, ed. J. Fentress. Sunderland, MA: Sinauer Associates.

Marler, P. (1984). Song learning: Innate species differences in the learning process. In *The biology of learning*, ed. P. Marler and H. S. Terrace. New York: Springer-Verlag.

Marler, P. (1987). Sensitive periods and the role of specific and general sensory stimulation in birdsong learning. In *Imprinting and cortical plasticity*, ed. J. P. Rauschecker and P. Marler. New York: John Wiley & Sons.

Marler, P, and Peters, S. (1980). Birdsong and speech: Evidence for special processing. In *Perspectives on the study of speech*, ed. P. Eimas and J. Miller. Hillsdale, NJ: Lawrence Erlbaum Associates.

Marler, P. and Peters, S. (1982a). Developmental overproduction and selective attrition: New processes in the epigenesis of birdsong. *Dev. Psychobiol.* 15:369–78.

Marler, P., and Peters, S. (1982b). Subsong and plastic song: Their role in the vocal learning process. In *Ecology and evolution of acoustic communication in birds*, Vol. 2, ed. D. E. Kroodsma, and E. H. Miller. New York: Academic Press.

Marler, P., and Peters S. (1987). A sensitive period for song acquisition in the song sparrow *Melospiza melodia:* A case of age-limited learning. *Ethology* 76:89–100.

Marler, P., and Peters, S. (1988a). Sensitive periods for song acquisition from tape recordings and live tutors in the swamp sparrow, *Melospiza georgiana. Ethology* 77:76–84.

Marler, P., and Peters, S. (1988b). The role of song phonology and syntax in vocal learning preferences in the song sparrow, *Melospiza melodia. Ethology* 77:125–49.

Marler, P., and Peters, S. (1989). Species differences in auditory responsiveness in early vocal learning. In *The Comparative psychology of audition: Perceiving complex sounds*, ed. S. Hulse and R. Dooling. Hillsdale, NJ: Lawrence Erlbaum Associates.

Marler, P., and Pickert, R. (1984). Species-universal microstructure in the learned song of the swamp sparrow *(Melospiza georgiana). Anim. Behav.* 32:673–89.

Marler, P., and Sherman, V. (1983). Song structure without auditory feedback: Emendations of the auditory template hypothesis. *J. of Neurosci.* 3:517–31.

Marler, P., and Sherman, V. (1985). Innate differences in singing behaviour of sparrows reared in isolation from adult conspecific song. *Anim. Behav.* 33:57–71.

Searcy W. A., and Marler, P. (1987). Response of sparrows to songs of deaf and isolation-reared males: Further evidence for innate auditory templates. *Dev. Psychobiol.* 20:509–20.

Tinbergen, N. (1951). *The study of instinct*. Oxford: Clarendon Press.

Chapter 7

Plasticity of Cortical Development

Pasko Rakic

Objectives

The goal of this chapter is to provide a model of the plasticity of cortical development. The human cerebral cortex is believed to be the organ of all the higher cognitive functions in man, including perception, memory, language, and abstract reasoning. Yet we know little about the factors controlling the development of this marvelous structure. The critical questions raised in this chapter involve the potential for plasticity associated with cortical development in primates as well as identification of the cellular mechanisms underlying this plasticity.

The data presented here are based on published work as well as the results of unpublished research from my laboratory and were derived both from animal experiments (i.e., rhesus monkeys) as well as from studies of postmortem human brain tissue.

Cortical Organization between and within Species

Figure 7.1 is a set of maps of the lateral and medial surface of the cerebral cortex for rats, rhesus monkeys, and humans, labeled numerically according to the system first invented by Brodmann (1904). Several points related to this figure bear mentioning. First, homologous cytoarchitectonic areas can be identified in diverse mammalian species, thus providing a basis for using nonhuman mammals as model systems for studying cortical organization. Second, the relative size and development of cortical areas vary between different species, reflecting the effects of natural selection. Finally, new cytoarchitectonic cortical areas have arisen in the course of primate and human evolution, consistent with the view that the potential for cortical organizational plasticity is substantial. In the next paragraphs I will discuss the significance of these points.

Even a causal inspection of figure 7.1 reveals that the size of the cortical surface area has been particularly enlarged in the primates. This expansion is not uniform, however. Rather, there has been se-

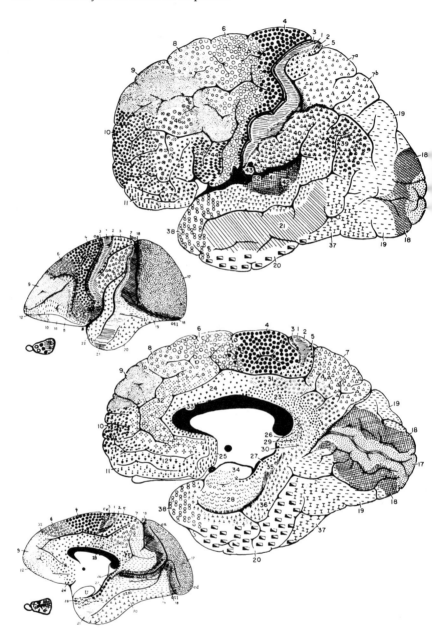

Figure 7.1
Lateral (upper figures) and medial (lower figures) view of the cerebral hemisphere in human (right) and macaque monkey (left) with schematic designation of individual cytoarchitectonic areas. Reproduced to approximate scale from Brodmann (1909).

lective expansion of specific cytoarchitectonic fields within the cortex of different primate species. For example, area 17, the primary visual cortex, constitutes 15 percent of the cortical surface in rhesus monkeys but only about 3 percent of the cortical surface in humans, although in absolute terms, the human has nearly the same amount of cortical surface apportioned to area 17 as the monkey.

Not only is the relative development of cortical areas different among primates, new cortical areas have appeared in the course of evolution. In the human for example, cortical areas for speech and language can be identified that are not present in monkeys. Finally, substantial differences in cortical organization can be identified among members of the same species, including siblings. Perhaps most surprising of all, we can identify differences between cortical areas located in the left and right cerebral hemispheres of the same individual. Pertinent to this, Geschwind and his colleagues have shown that the *planum temporale* is larger in the left than in the right hemisphere (Geschwind and Galaburda 1986). Thus there has been an expansion of cortical size in human evolution, along with the emergence of specialized and lateralized functional areas such as those related to speech and language.

The existence of such great diversity in the organization of the cerebral cortex both among and within mammalian species poses an intriguing problem for the developmental neurobiologist: How is this diversity generated? Are the total number of neurons for each cortical area in each hemisphere of each individual determined exclusively by genetic specification, or are other factors called into play during embryonic life that determine the ultimate size and internal structure of each cortical area? Further, can changes in the conditions associated with the embryonic life alter the patterns of cortical development and if so, how?

Although these questions are simple enough to state, they remained nearly insoluble until very recently, because the tools to answer such questions have only been available within the last two decades. These tools include powerful neuroanatomical techniques that allow neurobiologists to study neuronal formation, connectivity, histochemistry, immunocytochemistry and *in situ* hybridization. Among the tools one should also mention the possibilities of studying cell lineages by retrovirus-mediated gene transfer. Such methods allow us to go well beyond earlier studies based on examination of human post-mortem material and provide a means for studying the cortex as a network of interconnected neurons with chemical and hodological specificity. Finally, in contrast to earlier studies the new methods involve experimental manipulation and animal models by prenatal neurosurgery (Rakic and Goldman-Rakic 1985).

Experimental Studies of Cortical Organization

In order to answer the questions posed above concerning the factors controlling cortical growth and development, it was first necessary to learn more about the basic organization and connectivity of cortical neurons. Much of my research, as well as that of others, has been directed to this problem. The goal of these experiments has been to unravel the pattern of cortical connectivity—in other words to determine the patterns of interconnection of neurons in different cortical layers with other cortical neurons and with those in subcortical structures. Although difficult to work out, these problems have proven amenable to experimental study and have been largely successful. Thus we now know a great deal about the intrinsic organization of the primate cortex. This information provides a starting point for studies of cortical ontogeny and plasticity of development.

Figure 7.2 is a schematic diagram depicting neuronal sizes and morphology in each layer of the primary visual cortex (called area 17 by Brodmann). It was precisely this type of data that Brodmann used to construct his maps, and it was on the basis of this type of data that he identified specific cortical areas. The drawings in figure 7.2A illustrate the orientation of the dendrites and axons of neurons as well as the cell types and neuronal densities in each cortical layer. Since much of my research has concerned the development of visual area 17, this is a logical starting point for a discussion of cortical organization and ontogeny.

Brodmann recognized six cortical layers, each with a different pattern of neuronal types and densities, as shown in figure 7.2 Some of these layers are divided further into sublayers (layers IVA, IVB, IVC) On the basis of slight differences in neuronal sizes, densities, and orientation of neuronal processes (that is, dendritic arbors and axonal branching patterns). Altogether Brodmann recognized a total of 52 cortical areas based on these methods, although only about 47 are still used.

Note that Brodmann's work was basically descriptive; the methods used involved staining normal neurons and fibers using silver staining methods developed by neuroanatomists such as Golgi and Cajal. Although these techniques allow us to glimpse the nature of the cortical wiring diagram, such methods cannot specify precisely which neurons are connected together, since a large number of crisscrossing fibers are stained at the same time. Thus we can trace an axon a short

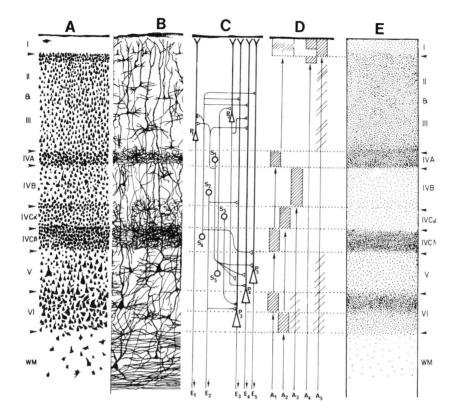

Figure 7.2

Composite diagram of the laminar organization of the primary visual cortex of the rhesus monkey, integrating observations derived by several techniques (modified from Rakic, Gallager, and Goldman-Rakic 1988). A: Cytoarchitectonic appearance of the primary visual cortex (area 17) in Nissl stain displaying horizontal cell stratification into layers and sublayers. B: Appearance of visual cortex neurons in Golgi impregnations and afferent axonal plexules in sublayers stained by the reduced silver method. C: Simplified diagram of the origin and termination of major neuronal circuits within the cortex. It is evident that stellate cells of sublayers IVCβ (S4) and IVA (S1) project predominantly to layer III, where they synapse either directly upon dendrites of efferent pyramidal cells (P1 and P2) or indirectly through another local circuit neuron (small pyramidal cell P2). The majority of stellate cells of sublayer IVCα (e.g., S3) probably contact efferent pyramids (P3) within layer V. Some stellate cells of layer IVβ (S2) contact nearby neurons within the same layer but also project to adjacent visual association cortex (E2). However, most visual efferents are formed by large pyramids (P3-5) of layer V, which project to the superior colliculus (E3); pyramids of upper layers VI (P4), which project to the parvocellular moiety of the lateral geniculate nucleus (E4); and pyramids of lower VI (P5), which project to the magnocellular moiety (E5). D: Relative position of the terminal field originating from five major afferent systems: A1 (from the parvocellular moiety of LGd), A2 (from the magnocellular moiety of LGd), A3 (from the superior temporal cortex), A4 (from the inferior pulvinar), and A5 (from area 18). E: Distribution of the alpha-2-adrenergic receptor as exposed by 3H-clonidine binding in area 17. (From Rakic et al. 1988.)

distance as it emerges from a neuron cell body with these methods, but we cannot follow it over a longer distance and cannot be sure where the axon ultimately terminates.

These technical problems have only recently been solved. During the last two decades new methods have been perfected that allow us to map out the patterns of connectivity of individual cortical neurons with a high degree of accuracy. Some of the examples of these pioneering studies are presented in figure 7.2C. As can be seen in this figure, the true wiring diagram of the primate cortex is quite complex. Rather than describe all of the known properties of cortical neuronal connectivity, I will concentrate on basic principles of cortical organization and how these organizational features arise during development.

Sublayer-Specific Projections of Cortical Neurons

The single most important principle of cortical organization identified by modern research is the fact that the depth of a neuron in the cortical sheet (the layer or sublayer it is contained in) allows us to predict its projections. Our knowledge of the efferent projections of a neuron (the outputs of a neuron conveyed via its axon) are so detailed, we can predict neuronal efferents for cells in each sublayer of the cortex. Three basic types of sublayer-specific neuronal projection patterns have been described. First, neurons primarily in the deeper layers (layers V and VI) project to subcortical targets. More specifically, cells of the lower part of layer VI project to the magnocellular part of the lateral geniculate nucleus in the thalamus, whereas cells of the upper part project to the parvocellular part of the same nucleus. Second, pyramidal neurons in the most superficial layers (layers I–III) project outside if the local cortical area to more distant cortical areas. Some of these cells also project to the contralateral hemisphere via the corpus callosum. Finally, some cortical neurons project primarily to other neurons located in the same local area. These may be found throughout the cortex but are concentrated mainly in layer IV.

In addition to the specificity of efferent projections, we can predict the distribution of terminals from afferent projections (sources of inputs received on the cell body, dendrites, or axon terminals) of a cortical neuron based on its laminar position. As for neuronal efferent connections, afferent inputs to the cortex are also sublayer specific. This is an extremely important finding since it provides a basis for evaluating the organization of different cortical areas both during and after development.

Most of the data in figures 7.2C and 7.2D are obtained by the use of an enzyme tracer, horseradish peroxidase (HRP). This enzyme is used as a tracer by direct injection into specific cortical regions. It is then taken up by nerve terminals present in the vicinity of the injection site and transported retrogradely (backward from the nerve terminals) to cortical cell bodies. In the example provided in figure 7.2C, deep situated neurons in layer VI would be labeled (filled with the enzyme marker) when this tracer is injected into the magnocellular portion of the lateral geniculate nucleus of the thalamus. Other neurons in layers above would be unlabeled by this injection, thus illustrating the sublayer specificity of cortical projections to this thalamic nucleus.

In the last ten years other retrograde tracing methods have been introduced that include fluorescent and other natural dyes. In addition anterograde tracing methods have also been developed. These markers are taken up by cell bodies and transported throughout a neuron including all branches and terminals of the axon. This method enables precise delineation of terminal fields for various afferents to the cortex as illustrated in figure 7.2D. Combined use of retrograde and anterograde transport marker methods has resulted in a virtual revolution in the field of neuroanatomy. We are now able to provide highly detailed maps of neuronal connectivity such as those illustrated in figure 7.2.

In addition to retrograde and anterograde pathway tracing methods, we now have *immunohistochemical techniques* available that allow us to specify the neurotransmitters utilized by neurons. An example of cells labeled by this method is illustrated in figure 7.3, in which a local circuit neuron (a spiny stellate neuron in layer IV) is treated with antibodies raised against a putative neurotransmitter-like substance called neuropeptide Y. This staining method allows us to determine unambiguously that this particular neuron contains and presumably utilizes neuropeptide Y in synaptic transmission. Physiological studies show that neuropeptide Y has an excitatory function in the cortex. Double labeling with an antibody for gamma aminobuteric acid (GABA) shows that some cells have more than one transmitter and that some of them can have an opposite effect (that is, an inhibitory effect). Note that the axon of the cell is also stained with the antibody. These immunohistochemical methods thus also provide a way to map out neuronal connectivity. When combined with anatomical pathway-tracing techniques as described, these methods enable us to specify the projections and neurotransmitter characteristics of neurons and their synaptic circuits.

We now also have methods at our disposal that tell us about the receptors associated with the neurotransmitters and modulators released at cortical synapses. Since virtually all synaptic connections

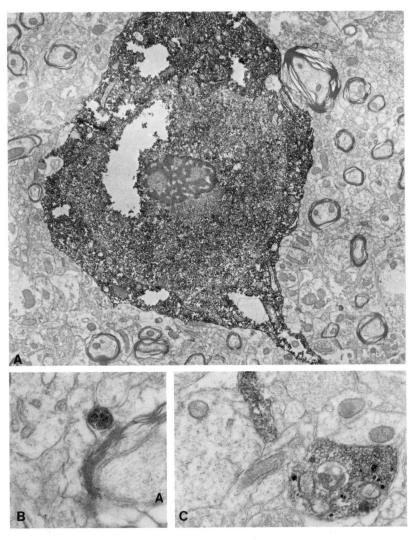

Figure 7.3
A: Electron micrograph of the perikaryon of the neuropeptide Y (NPY)-containing cell located in the dorsal bank of the principal sulcus. Most cytoplasmic organelles appear heavily labeled, except mitochondrdia. B: transverse section of a labeled unmyelinated axon (center and up). Notice that the labeled axon forms a bundle with unstained, unmyelinated axons. C: presynaptic profile contacting unlabeled dendrites forming symmetric synapses. (From Kuljis and Rakic 1989.)

utilize chemical transmitter substances, receptors must exist by which these chemical transmitters exert their effects. These receptors can be identified through the use of ligand-binding techniques in which radioactive ligands are used to label receptor sites in the cortical sheet. The use of such a method (called receptor-binding autoradiography) is illustrated in figures 7.2E and 7.4. In the latter case the distribution of serotonergic receptor sites was mapped using radioactively labeled serotonin as the ligand (Rakic, Gallager, and Goldman-Rakic 1988). The presence of the ligand was determined by pressing tissue sections, which had been previously dipped in a solution containing the radioactively labeled ligand, against a highly sensitive X-ray film. Radioactivity in the tissue thus was used to expose the film and produce an image of the patterns of binding sites for serotonin (and by implication for the distribution of serotonergic receptors). The films were then analyzed by a computer densitometry system. As for the pathway tracing and immunohistochemical methods, ligand-binding sites can be mapped specific to the sublayer, thus providing yet another tool for characterizing cortical organization and structure. Furthermore these receptor-binding methods can be used to answer questions related to development. For example, we can correlate the appearance of these receptors at different stages of cortical development with other aspects of cortical structure and connectivity.

As a result of the use of these new techniques the developmental neurobiologist must now grapple with a far greater data base than Brodmann used to make his original maps. Cortical complexity is currently understood not only in terms of cytoarchitecture but in terms of the interconnections of neurons, the development of receptors, and the development of the chemical systems that mediate synaptic transmission. The problem is further complicated by the fact that these patterns are quite different in different cortical areas. For example, the distribution of most receptors in area 18 is different than the distribution in area 17 of the visual cortex. Thus layers IV and VI in figure 7.4 are heavily labeled in area 17, but the pattern of serotonin receptors is less distinct in area 18. Note also that the pattern in area 17 ends abruptly at the border with area 18.

Many interesting questions pertinent to the study of cortical development arise from these studies. For example, does the abrupt change in the pattern of serotonin innervation and receptor distribution between areas 17 and 18 appear early in cortical development, or is it induced by functional activity as the cortex grows and develops? At what stage of cortical development does this chemoarchitectonic feature first appear, and what factors are responsible for its appearance? Is this feature genetically determined, or is it determined by environ-

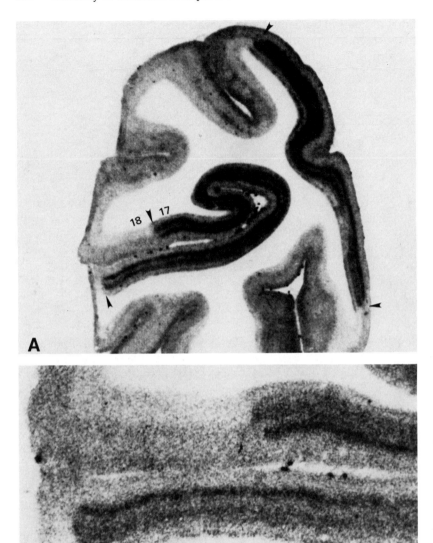

Figure 7.4
A: Low-power video image of 3H-5-HT binding sites showing the sharp change in distribution of radioactivity at the borderline between areas 17 and 18 (arrowheads) in the adult rhesus monkey. *In vitro* binding of the radioligand provides a reliable means of identifying the size of cytoarchitectonic fields and location of their borders. B: Higher-power autoradiogram of the 17/18 border and lamination pattern within the calcarine fissure. (From Rakic et al. 1988.)

mental signals in the embryo? Finally, how are these cortical features correlated with the development of brainstem serotonin neurons, including other projections of these neurons? The same questions can be repeated for other receptors as well, including dopaminergic, adrenergic, glutaminergic, and GABAergic receptors.

Development of the Cortex

Neurogenesis

The starting point for my research in cortical development was the development and implementation of a set of methods that enable us to determine when each cortical neuron is generated for each cortical area. Using these methods, we have been able to determine, quite literally, the "birthday" of each cortical neuron as well as some information about the history of all neurons destined to become part of the cerebral cortex (Rakic 1974).

The key to answering these questions lies in the use of a tracer technique using a radioactively labeled nucleotide, tritiated thymidine. This method allows us to determine the day upon which the final cell division that produced a particular neuron took place. This is because thymidine is taken up by cells actively synthesizing DNA. Although many cells in the body continue to grow and divide throughout life, neurons do not (Rakic 1985a). Thus an injection of tritiated thymidine into an embryo will only label cells undergoing cell division. Fully formed neurons will not be labeled. The greatest accumulation of labels will be in cells taking up the tracer during their last cell division (so that there will be no further dilution of the tracer during the life of the cell). Using this method, it has proven possible to construct maps of the birthdays of neurons in each layer of the cortex for many cortical areas. Tritiated thymidine is radioactive, and its presence in neurons is demonstrated autoradiographically as shown in figure 7.5 (from Rakic 1988).

In our research we have worked mostly with rhesus monkeys. Therefore our discussion concerning the birthdates of neurons applies to the monkey brain, and by implication to primates in general. Our protocols involved injecting tritiated thymidine into pregnant female rhesus monkeys at different points during gestation (i.e., at different points in the embryonic development of their fetus). Although rhesus monkeys are quite different from humans in many respects, they provide an excellent model for cortical development. This is because the structure of the cortex, including the sublayer organization and neuronal projections, is similar to that of humans and has been specified quite precisely, as I have discussed above. Thus we can use

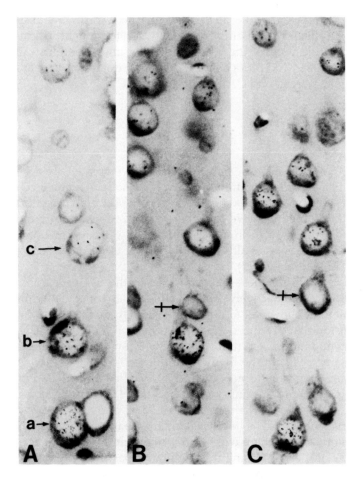

Figure 7.5
Microphotograph of the three autoradiograms showing neurons in the cortex of an adult monkey that was exposed to [3H] thymidine at embryonic day 70. A: The most intensely radioactive neuron (a) lies deeper in the cortex than the two progressively less labeled, more superficially situated neurons (b and c). B and C: Unlabeled neurons (crossed arrows) may be interspersed among radioactive neurons within the same ontogenetic column. Further explanation is in the text. (From Rakic 1988.)

rhesus monkeys to define the basic principles of cortical neurogenesis and development.

Figure 7.6 provides an illustration of the results of a series of experiments in which tritiated thymidine was injected into rhesus mothers at different points during fetal development. For example, if a pulse of thymidine is injected on the 50th day of embryonic life (E50) of the fetus, labeled cortical cells will be present *exclusively* in layer 6. For all cortical areas examined, cells in layer 6 form first. On the other hand if thymidine is injected on embryonic day E70, a different population of cortical cells are labeled. The results are summarized in the top portion of figure 7.6 for a limbic cortical area (area 24) and in the bottom portion of figure 7.6 for the striate cortex (area 17). Note that different populations of cortical neurons are generated on each day of embryonic life and that the patterns of neurogenesis are not identical for the two cortical areas illustrated (see figure 7.6). Furthermore all cortical neurons are generated in the first half of pregnancy (see figure 7.6). This means that the second half of pregnancy involves the formation of synaptic connections, not additional cortical neurogenesis.

We cannot use tritiated thymidine to study human cortical development, nevertheless information obtained from examination of human postmortem fetal brain material has provided results consistent with those obtained in monkeys by experimental methods. As in monkeys, all human cortical neurons are generated during the first half of pregnancy. As you read this chapter, you might reflect on the fact that all the cortical neurons you are using to process the information contained here were produced during the first 17 weeks of your fetal life.

Certain generalizations concerning cortical neurogenesis can be made based on our research. First, we have found that for all cortical areas examined neurons in the deeper layers of the cortex always form first. As I have described, these are the neurons that project to subcortical structures such as the thalamus. Next local circuit neurons in the middle layers form. Neurons in the superficial cortical layers, which project outside local areas of cortex, are the last to form. Functionally this means that circuits connecting the cortex with subcortical structures form first. Then cortical local circuit neurons form. Finally neurons capable of supporting cortico-cortical circuits form. These patterns are highly consistent and found for all cortical areas.

Since we can determine the exact time a particular neuron in a particular layer of a given cortical area is formed, we can determine when neurons associated with specific chemical systems are formed. For example, the neuron illustrated in figure 7.3, labeled with antibodies raised against neuropeptide-Y, is located in layer 3. These neurons

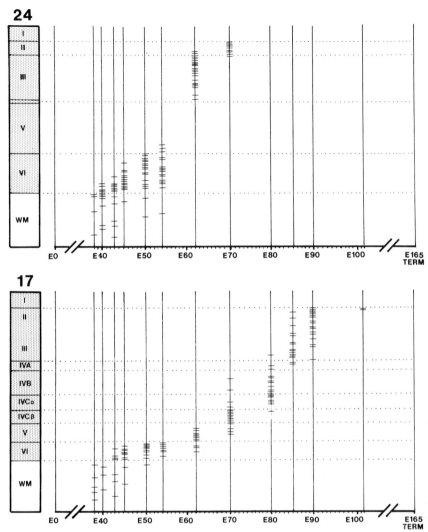

Figure 7.6
Diagrammatic representation of the positions of heavily labeled neurons in the cortex of juvenile monkeys, each of which had been injected with 3H-thymidine at selected embryonic days: top, area 24; bottom, area 17 of Brodmann (1909). On the left side of each diagram is a drawing of the cortex from cresyl-violet-stained sections, in which subdivisions into cortical layers are indicated by Roman numerals. Embryonic days (E) are represented on the horizontal line, starting on the left with the end of the first fetal month (E27) and ending on the right at term (E165). Positions of vertical lines (A to R) indicate the embryonic day on which one animal received a pulse of 3H-TdR. On each vertical line, short horizontal markers indicate positions of all heavily labeled neurons encountered in one 2.5 mm-long strip of cortex. Abbreviations: LV, obliterated posterior horn of the lateral ventricle; WM, white matter. (From Rakic 1974, 1976.)

are born on embryonic day 80, along with other spiny stellate cells in this sublayer of monkey visual cortex. Thus we can determine the birth date of each neuron type as defined by its morphology, neuro-transmitter content, receptor characteristics, and anatomical projections. Such techniques allows us to describe cortical morphogenesis in a way that was undreamed of only a short time ago and provide a powerful set of tools that enable us to understand the dynamics of cortical growth and development during embryonic life.

The top of figure 7.6 provides a map of cortical birth dates for a portion of the cortex called the limbic cortex. This area corresponds to the region forming the anterior cingulate gyrus and was termed area 24 by Brodmann. Notice that few cells in this cortical area are born on embryonic day 70 (a time when many cells are forming in the visual cortex). None are generated after E70. Thus cortical neurogenesis is not a uniform process. Each cortical area tends to develop during a specific time window, and although there is overlap, only selected portions of the cortex are undergoing significant neurogenesis at a given time during embryonic life.

This finding has significance in human medicine and provides us with a way to interpret studies of the effects of teratogens on human fetal brain development. Teratogens are substances or stimuli that interfere with embryonic development, such as drugs, viruses, environmental toxins, and ionizing radiation (X-rays, gamma rays, etc.). Since the disruptive effects of a teratogen will be experienced at the time the agent interacts with fetal tissue, the effects of teratogens on cortical development can be predicted from the studies of the patterns of cortical neurogenesis. Put simply cortical neurons will be at greatest risk when they are actively proliferating. Neurons already formed will show the least susceptibility to teratogenic effects. Depending on the gestational age of the fetus, teratogens may completely disrupt the development of cortical areas undergoing rapid neuronal proliferation, while sparing other areas completely. For example, on embryonic day 70, as illustrated in figure 7.6, the effect of a teratogen for the developing rhesus will be slight for layer 2 of limbic cortex, but quite severe for layer 4 of primary visual cortex.

Migration of Neuroblasts
The next point that needs to be made is that, remarkably, none of these cortical neurons are actually produced in the cortex. Instead these neurons are generated in a narrow site closely apposed to the ventricle from which they migrate into the cortical mantle. This process is shown in figure 7.7A, which illustrates a cell showing a mitotic figure. (A mitotic figure represents chromosomal segregation during

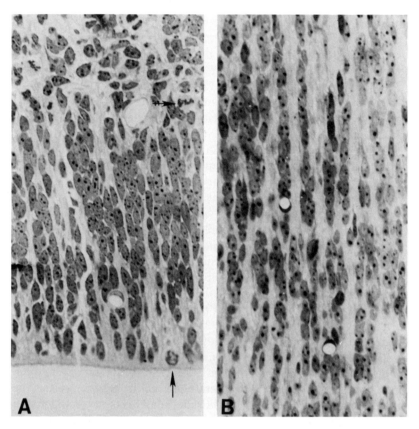

Figure 7.7
Radial organization of both ventricular zone and fetal cortical plate are best visible in the cresyl-violet-stained sections. A: Photomicrograph of an array of proliferative units within the ventricular zone of the occipital lobe in a 91-day-old monkey embryo. Most mitotic figures are located directly at the ventricular surface (arrow), although at this age some can be found in the subventricular zone (crossed arrow). B: Cortical plate in the occipital lobe of the same animal showing ontogenetic columns composed of neurons that have originated from the set of proliferative units illustrated in A. Epon-embedded tissue, cut at 1 um, stained with cresyl violet. (From Rakic 1988b.)

cell division.) This cell is actively dividing and producing daughter cells. Once generated, the daughter cells migrate and move into the cortex, where they accumulate. In a small animal such as a mouse or a rat, the distance involved is small, however, in a human, the distance becomes quite large as the cortex thickens and the brain enlarges. This raises a new question: How does this migration occur despite the existence of considerable space in the primate brain between the ventricular surface and the cortical plate?

The cell showed in figure 7.7 is located along the ventricular surface near the calcarine fissure. All of the neurons that will come to occupy sites within the primary visual cortex are born here and must migrate a distance of over 5 millimeters from this narrow zone into the cortical plate. Since the neurons themselves, including leading process, are only about 200 microns in longitudinal diameter, each must migrate over a large number of cellular diameters to reach their final destination.

Migration of neuroblasts from proliferative zones near the ventricular surface to the cortical plate in primates is made possible by the existence of specialized, transient, nonneural cells called *radial glial cells* (Rakic 1972). Figure 7.8 illustrates the manner in which radial glial cells provide an enabling mechanism for migration of cortical neuroblasts. As shown in this figure, the radial glia extend processes from the ventricular surface to the surface of the cortex and act, in effect, as a highway by which migrating neuroblasts find their way to sites within the cortical mantle.

Radial glia are specialized, nonneuronal cells that exist only during embryonic life. We can prove that radial glia are not neurons in several ways. First, we can use the Golgi stain to visualize the morphology of these cells. (Refer back to figure 7.2 for examples of the use of silver stains such as the Golgi stain for visualizing neuronal morphology.) Second, we can use electron microscopy to study the structure of radial glia. Electron microscopic studies show that radial glial cells are quite different ultrastructurally from neurons (Rakic 1972, 1985b). Finally, we can use an immunohistochemical method, in which a glial-specific monoclonal antibody is used to stain these radial glia (Levitt, Cooper, and Rakic 1981). This immunohistochemical method has the added advantage of providing a way of proving that the radial glial cells exist only in the embryo and disappear when cortical neurogenesis is completed (Schmechel and Rakic 1979).

Using these methods, we can prove that during early embryonic life two cell populations are present in the developing cortex—glial and neuronal. The glia include the transient radial glia, which disappear after cortical morphogenesis and serve as guides for neurons migrating from the ventricular surface to their ultimate destinations

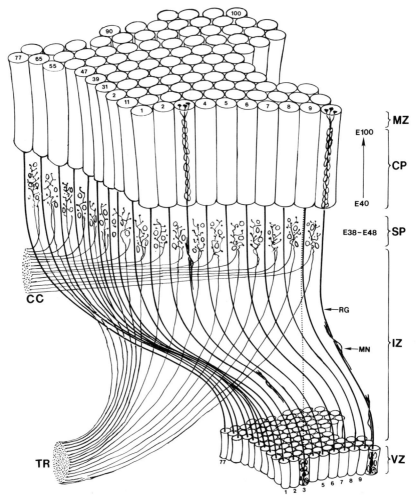

Figure 7.8
The relation between a small patch of the proliferative, ventricular zone (VZ) and its corresponding area within the cortical plate (CP) in the developing cerebrum. Although the cerebral surface in primates expands and shifts during prenatal development, ontogenetic columns (outlined by cylinders) remain attached to the corresponding proliferative units by the grid of radial glial fibers. Neurons produced between E40 and E100 by a given proliferative unit migrate in succession along the same radial glial guides (RG) and stack up in reverse order of arrival within the same ontogenetic column. Each migrating neuron first traverses the intermediate zone (IZ) and then the subplate (SP), which contains interstitial cells, waiting afferents from the thalamic radiation (TR), and ipsilateral and contralateral cortico-cortical connections (CC). After entering the cortical plate, each neuron bypasses earlier-generated neurons and settles at the interface between the CP and marginal zone (MZ). As a result, proliferative units 1 to 100 produce ontogenetic columns 1 to 100 in the same relative position to each other without a lateral mismatch (for example, between proliferative unit 3 and ontogenetic column 9, indicated by a dashed line). Thus the specification of cytoarchitectonic areas and topographic maps depends on the spatial distribution of their ancestors in the proliferative units, while the laminar position and phenotype of neurons within ontogenetic columns depends on the time of their origin (from Rakic 1988b).

in specific sublayers of cortical areas. Several laboratories including ours are currently trying to find out more about this process by applying cell biological methods to identify the surface molecules on the glial cells and neurons that provide a mechanism for adhesion, enabling neurons to use glial cells as migratory guides during development (Hatten and Mason 1986; Mason and Hatten 1985; Rakic 1985b; Schachner et al. 1985; Cunningham et al. 1986). The importance of this problem lies in the fact that migration determines the distribution of neuronal types within sublayers of specific cytoarchitectonic cortical areas and therefore determines the functional organization of the cortex.

Constraints on Migration Patterns
There are two major questions that can be raised at this point. The first is related to the vertical movement of neuroblasts along the radial glia. Simply put, we can ask, What stops migration and determines which layer a neuron will occupy? The second question involves constraints on the lateral movement of neuroblasts. The issue here concerns the restrictiveness of the migratory patterns of particular neurons into specific cortical areas.

A dramatic example of the importance of these processes in determining cortical structure is provided by a recent postmortem study of the brains of humans whose mothers were exposed to high levels of radiation due to the atomic explosions at Hiroshima and Nagasaki (Otake and Shull 1984). Remarkably, about 80 percent of the cases in which the individuals had been mentally retarded had been irradiated during weeks 10 to 17 of gestational life (that is, the mothers were exposed during 10 to 17 weeks of pregnancy). The reason for this is that it is precisely during this period of gestational life (between 10 and 17 weeks) that the second wave of cortical migration occurs, giving rise to neurons that migrate into the superficial layers of the cortex (Rakic 1978; Sidman and Rakic 1982). As mentioned above, cells in superficial cortical layers normally give rise to cortico-cortical projections, but radiation prevented these cortical layers from forming. As a result these individuals had sufficient brain function to survive to birth, yet lacked normal cortical functioning and showed severe mental retardation. X-ray irradiation of the monkey fetus at midgestation produces the same effect (Rakic and Goldman-Rakic unpublished observation). Thus we have an experimental model to test the mechanism of cortical malformation that mimics the situation in humans.

Dramatic confirmation of this hypothesis was provided by direct examination of the brain of a 16-year-old victim of the Hiroshima explosion who was irradiated on week 11 of gestation. Compared to a normal brain, the superficial cortical layers were essentially absent, the corpus callosum was thin, and, most remarkable of all, many unmigrated neurons could be observed near the wall of the ventricle. These cells never migrated from their proliferative zones because the radial glia that would have provided a mechanism for migration were destroyed by the radiation. This provides dramatic confirmation of the fact that the radial glia are essential for vertical migration of neuroblasts in humans as well as in monkeys.

Ontogenetic Columns
The preceding discussion has concerned the vertical migration of cortical neuroblasts from the ventricular wall to the cortical mantle. Our research on the functions of radial glia also provides information about the factors controlling the lateral movement of cortical neurons. As shown in figure 8, lateral movement of migrating cortical neurons is severely constrained by the physical relationship between neurons and glia resulting from the adhesive properties of the neuron-glial membrane attachment mechanism. Thus neurons that are generated close together near the ventricular wall must follow similar paths and will ultimately reach the same small patch of cortex (Rakic 1988b).

The deeper layers of the cortex form first. Those occupying the superficial layers form later. As a result, the cortex is generated by a kind of inside-outside pattern (Rakic 1974). Despite this pattern, however, all the neurons in a column extending from the cortical surface to the white matter will have been generated from germinal cells located in the same small proliferative region near the ventricle of the embryonic forebrain due to the action of the neuron-radial glial attachment process. For these reasons we refer to such closely associated bundles of radial glial fibers as *ontogenetic columns* (Rakic 1978, 1988b). The zone within the ventricular layer giving rise to all of the neurons of a specified ontogenetic column is called a *proliferative unit*. Each proliferative unit is associated with an ontogenetic column. As a result lateral migration of cortical neurons is severely constrained.

These patterns and cell relationships are very clear in the embryo but are more difficult to recognize in the adult cortex due to the disappearance of the radial glia and subsequent loss of the distinct boundaries of embryonic ontogenetic columns. Nevertheless the organization of the cortex is largely determined by these migratory patterns, and the circuitry of adult cortex reflects the columnar pattern of organization that was laid down during embryonic life (Rakic 1988b).

Each ontogenetic column contains 100 to 120 neurons. In the monkey the entire cortex of a single hemisphere contains about 20 to 25 million such columns (Rakic 1988b). At present we have only a rough estimate of the number of such columns in humans; however, we believe that the one hemisphere of the human cortex contains approximately 300 million such columns.

Experimental Manipulation of the Development of Ocular Dominance Columns in Area 17

The size of each cortical area reflects the number of proliferative units that contributed to it (Rakic 1988b). For example, in monkey primary visual cortex (area 17), almost equal numbers of proliferative units produce approximately 2 1/2 million ontogenetic columns. We postulated that each cytoarchitectonic field is represented by area-specific proliferative units that form a provisionary map or *protomap* at the ventricular surface (Rakic 1988b). One of the questions we have raised in our research concerns the plasticity of this map. Could we manipulate the size of the cytoarchitectonic areas? In order to explore this possibility, we have used various experimental manipulations to alter the size of a given cortical area by changing the conditions obtaining in the embryonic brain.

Most of our research on cortical developmental plasticity has focused on the primary visual cortex of the monkey (area 17). One reason for this is that we know a great deal about the neuroanatomical organization of area 17 in this species, including the distribution of afferent and efferent connections (Hubel and Wiesel 1977). Furthermore, the visual system is a particularly good model for studying developmental processes because a number of important experimental manipulations, such as enucleation (removal of an eye during embryonic life) or injection of tracers into the eye, are relatively easy to carry out and provide useful tools for studying the mechanisms underlying cortical development (Rakic 1976, 1977, 1981).

In primates area 17 receives a substantial input from the lateral geniculate nucleus of the thalamus. The lateral geniculate nucleus receives input from both retinae via the optic tracts. Input from both eyes projects to each lateral geniculate nucleus; however, inputs from the contralateral eye and ipsilateral eye are segregated into different layers within each geniculate body. Ipsilateral input reaches geniculate layers 2, 3, and 5 while contralateral input reaches geniculate layers 1, 4, and 6. Neurons in all layers of the lateral geniculate nucleus project to area 17 of the cortex; however, the projections of geniculate layers overlap only partially within each cortical region, so that each patch of cortical tissue tends to respond mainly to the right eye, the left eye, or nearly equally to both eyes.

These cortical patches are called *ocular dominance columns* (Hubel, Wiesel, and LeVay 1977). Within each ocular dominance column all neurons from the cortical surface to the white matter tend to show the same pattern of selectivity for visual stimulation in each eye. Further, these patterns of ocular dominance alternate within area 17, forming a mosaic pattern throughout the cortex (see figure 7.9).

We can study the development of cortical ocular dominance columns by injecting radioactive tracers into the eyes during different stages of development and observing how many and which columns are labeled later (Rakic 1976, 1977). This method was used to produce the autoradiographs illustrated in figure 7.9. Note that the pattern is robust and readily visualized with the methods employed.

Using these methods, we have found that at an early stage of embryonic development the entire lateral geniculate body is labeled when the tracer is placed in only one eye (Rakic 1976) (see figure 7.10). As development proceeds the left and right eye inputs become segregated within different layers of the lateral geniculate body. A corre-

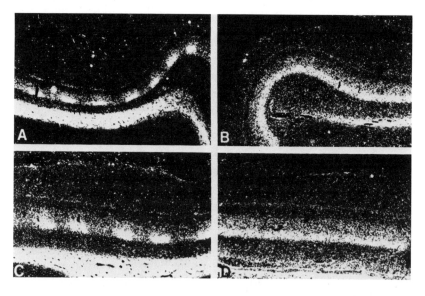

Figure 7.9
Dark-field illumination photomicrograph of autoradiograms showing the distribution of transneuronally transported radioactive tracers in the primary visual cortex of normal adult monkeys (A,C) and in adult monkeys whose one eye has been enucleated during the first third of pregnancy (B,D). Note the lack of alternating ocular dominance columns in the cortex of experimental animals. The distribution of silver grains over sublayers of layer IV remain similar to that in the control (from Rakic 1983).

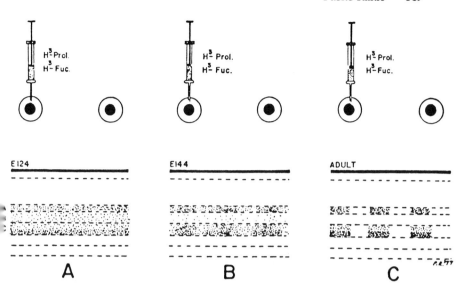

Figure 7.10
Schematic representation of the development of ocular dominance columns in layer 4 of the primary visual cortex of the rhesus monkey of various ages (E124, E144, adult) as visualized in autoradiograms following transneuronal transport of radioactive tracers (3H-fucose and 3H-proline) injected into one eye 14 days before sacrifice. Cortical layers indicated by numerals 1 through 6 are delineated according to Brodmann's (1909) classification. (Based on data from Rakic 1976, 1977.)

sponding process takes place in the cortex. At first ocular dominance patterns are not apparent in the cortex. Later the ocular dominance pattern begins to appear and becomes increasingly better defined as development proceeds (Rakic 1976, 1977).

The fact that segregation of retinal inputs within geniculate layers and cortical ocular dominance columns gradually develop during development of the visual system opens the possibility that at least some aspects of the development of central visual pathways are controlled by signals from the periphery. This means that neural pathways organize themselves substantially during development and that not all aspects of the developmental process are determined by genetic information contained within cortical neurons.

In attempting to explain our results, we focused on two possible hypotheses for the basis of this plasticity. The first possibility is that axons rearrange during development; the other possibility is that axons that have reached the wrong target or an inappropriate target are eliminated. Evidence favors the latter mechanism as the primary basis of developmental plasticity for the developing visual system, although both processes may be involved in the formation of the final pattern. This conclusion is based on the experiments that will be briefly described below, and they may be taken as an example of the more general process.

The optic nerve of an adult monkey has approximately 1.2 million fibers. Yet during embryonic life the monkey optic nerves have nearly twice this number of axons (Rakic and Riley 1983a). This is because optic axons are rapidly eliminated during the period when retinal inputs to the lateral geniculate layers become segregated and ocular dominance columns begin to appear within area 17 of the cortex. Therefore, both the segregation of optic inputs within the monkey visual thalamus and the subsequent development of well-defined ocular dominance columns within the visual cortex may be due to the elimination of an overabundance of axons projecting to an incorrect target (Rakic and Riley 1983a).

Counts of the number of axons in the human optic nerve at 16 weeks of human gestational age also show that the optic nerve has nearly three times as many axons as an adult human optic nerve (Provis et al. 1986). Thus the principle of elimination of axons projecting to the incorrect target appears to hold for humans as well as for monkeys. One of the general findings that we have obtained from our studies of brain development, particularly of cortical development, is that there is a great overproduction of neurons in the embryo. Those that project to incorrect or aberrant targets ultimately die and are eliminated.

In order to test this hypothesis, we used a different approach to the study of visual cortical plasticity. In this experiment one eye was enucleated early in development at a time when there was still considerable overlap between the projections of the optic tracts within the lateral geniculate nuclei. We were interested in how the projections of the remaining eye would map onto the thalamus and cortex. As shown in figure 7.11, all layers of the lateral geniculate body were invaded by retinal axons derived from the remaining eye (Rakic 1981). This is quite different from the normal case, in which each retina projects only to layers 1, 4, and 6 contralaterally and layers 2, 3, and 5 ipsilaterally.

The results of the experiment portrayed in figure 7.10 indicate that axons projecting to incorrect geniculate layers nevertheless persist following unilateral enucleation. We proposed that this persistence occurs because of a lack of competition that would normally take place between incorrectly projecting axons and those projecting to the correct targets (Rakic 1981). In other words, during embryonic life more neurons are normally produced than are needed, and the normal pat-

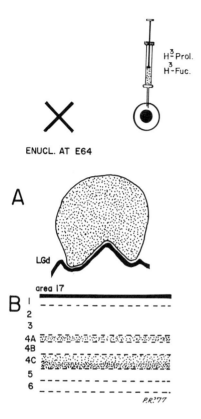

Figure 7.11
Schematic representation of the distribution of radioactive tracers in the LGd and primary visual cortex of a 2-month-old monkey 14 days after injection of a mixture of 3H-proline and 3H-fucose into one eye. In this animal the other eye had been removed on E64. The fetus was then returned to the uterus and delivered near term. Under these circumstances orthogradely transported radioactive label is distributed uniformly over the entire LGd, and transneuronally transported label forms a uniform band over sublayers 4A and 4C without a trace of alternating ocular dominance columns. (Based on data from Rakic 1977, 1979.)

tern of neuronal connectivity may be produced by a process in which cell death and axon degeneration result from competition between fibers projecting to the correct targets and those projecting to incorrect targets. In some way incorrect projections are weaker, or more susceptible to disruption by competition, and disappear as a result. Our finding that the remaining eye in adult monkeys monocularly enucleated as embryos contains larger numbers of retinal ganglion cells and optic fibers (Rakic and Riley 1983b) supports the concept of competition. In this case the remaining eye has more axons because it survives in the absence of competition from the contralateral eye (Rakic 1986).

In cases such as that illustrated in figure 7.11, in which unilateral enucleation was performed early in embryonic life, the laminar organization of the lateral geniculate is disrupted. This is because the remaining eye projects to all layers, and laminar differences, which are normally associated with segregation of inputs from the two eyes, fail to develop. Nevertheless the total number of neurons present in the lateral geniculate body remains unchanged. Similarly, although the striate cortex (area 17) fails to develop the normal pattern of ocular dominance columns, the overall size of the cortex does not change very much.

On the other hand, when both eyes are removed early in embryonic life, only about one-third of the normal number of neurons in the lateral geniculate nucleus survive (Rakic 1988b) (see figure 7.12). Furthermore the area 17 in these animals is also only about one-third of normal size. This fact indicates that the presence of retinal axons growing into the brain from the eye is necessary for maintaining the growth and development of the thalamic and cortical components of the visual pathway. Nevertheless, the remaining neurons in the lateral geniculate nucleus do indeed project to area 17, which indicates that some properties of the neurons in the lateral geniculate nucleus (such as projections to area 17) are retained in the absence of cues from the periphery. Moreover the cortical projections of these remaining geniculate neurons exhibit the normal pattern of topographic organization (that is, they project in a point-to-point manner), and they receive projections back from the cortex as is the case in normal animals (Rakic 1988b).

This does not mean that the visual cortex of monkeys sustaining bilateral enucleation in embryonic life is normal. As shown in figure 7.13, there are remarkable changes in the external morphology of the visual cortex in these animals when compared to that of normal monkeys. In addition to the loss of neurons described above, new convolutions and an unusual fold in the cortical surface appear in the cortex

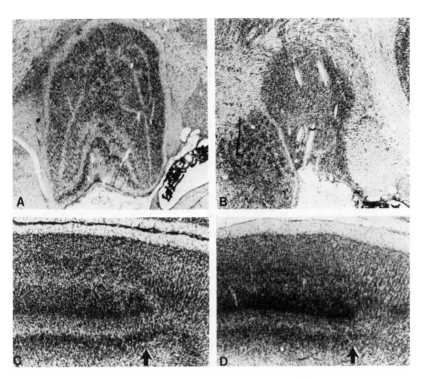

Figure 7.12
Photomicrograph of the lateral geniculate nucleus in (A) a normal rhesus monkey and
(B) its grossly diminished counterpart in the age-matched monkey subjected to binocular enucleation around E60. The border between the striate cortex (left) and extra-
striate cortex (right) in (C) a normal adult monkey and (D) an age-matched binocular
enucleate are marked with arrows. Photomicrographs A and B and photomicrographs
C and D are reproduced at the same magnification (from Rakic 1988b).

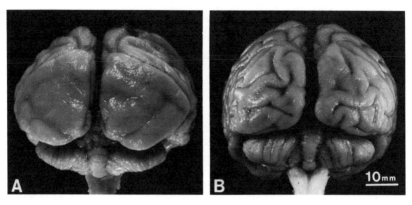

Figure 7.13
Posterior view of the cerebrum in (A) a normal 3-year-old monkey and (B) an age-matched animal that underwent bilateral enucleation at E60. The development of a new pattern of sulci and gyri is seen in the normally smooth lateral surface of the occipital lobe (from Rakic 1988).

of monkeys sustaining bilateral enucleation in embryonic life. Apparently there have been changes in the arrangement or patterning of the remaining cortical neurons.

As shown in figure 7.13, there is a remarkable reduction in the total size of the straite cortex (area 17) when both eyes are removed in embryonic life. In order to understand why this reduction occurs, we studied the patterns of cell migration and proliferation in embryos with bilateral enucleation. Three possible outcomes were envisaged at the start of these experiments (see figure 7.14). The number of ontogenetic columns could remain normal with fewer LGd neurons projecting to each column (reduced thickness of the columns as shown in figure 7.14B); the number and thickness of the columns could remain normal with the laminar organization disrupted (figure 7.14C); or the thickness and laminar organization could remain normal with a reduction in the number of columns (figure 7.14D).

The results showed, surprisingly, that there were fewer ontogenetic columns in these cases; however, each column had normal thickness and composition (Rakic 1988b), as depicted in figure 7.14D. Furthermore all layers and sublayers in the affected cortex were of approximately normal thicknesses. Computer quantification revealed approximately normal cell numbers and densities within the ontogenetic columns with approximately normal neuronal sizes (Rakic and Williams 1986). In other words, reduction in the size of area 17 in these cases reflects almost exclusively the presence of fewer ontoge-

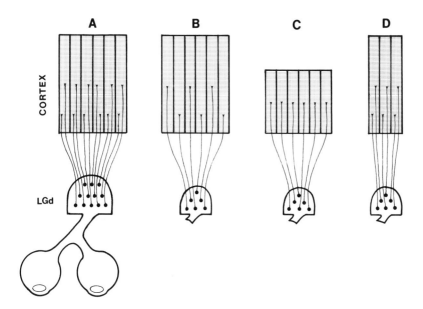

Figure 7.14
Schematic outline of the possible consequences of diminished input from the dorsal lateral geniculate nucleus (LGd) to the visual cortex in adults binocularly enucleated at early embryonic stages. The normal numerical relation between geniculocortical projections and ontogenetic columns illustrated in (A) can be altered in three basic ways (B, C, and D) that are discussed in the text (from Rakic 1988).

netic columns, rather than changes in the columns themselves or neurons in the columns.

In addition to normal neuronal sizes, densities, and laminar organization, area 17 showed normal synaptic density (Bourgeois and Rakic 1987). Finally, to our surprise, chemoarchitecture in these cases was also normal. For example, the normal pattern of rich serotonergic innervation in layer IV of area 17 is present in the cortices of enucleated monkeys, and other patterns of neurotransmitter and receptor organization are normal as well (Rakic et al. 1977). The principal effect of enucleation was a reduction in the number of ontogenetic columns with retention of normal cytoarchitecture, chemoarchitecture, and histology.

Having demonstrated that the magnitude of the thalamic input to a cortical area affects its ultimate size during development, we can ask whether other inputs also exert the same kinds of controlling effects on development via competition processes. In addition to thalamic inputs, cortical areas receive inputs from other subcortical nuclei, from other cortical areas in the same hemisphere, and from cortical areas in the contralateral hemisphere via the corpus callosum.

Pertinent to this, we have found that the number of axons in the corpus callosum is almost four times as great in a newborn monkey as it is in an adult monkey (LaMantia and Rakic 1990a). This suggests that competition and winnowing of cortico-cortical inputs does take place during early postnatal development. Based on these data and other studies, we estimate that as many as 60 axons per second are lost in the first few weeks of monkey life (see figure 7.15).

In the case of humans, the number of axons lost within the corpus callosum after birth may be even greater, approaching 200 axons per second during the first few weeks of life. This indicates that a considerable amount of competition and cell death takes place during early postnatal development as well as during embryonic life and that cell death and axon degeneration provides a basis for cortical developmental plasticity during at least the early portion of infancy. It is not yet known exactly which axon types are being eliminated during early infancy. We don't know, for example, if axon degeneration is derived from the same cortical regions for all individuals or if considerable individual differences exist during development with respect to which axon types are lost. Conceivably a child's early environment might be capable of determining the architecture of that individual's brain by influencing which axon types are eliminated in the corpus callosum.

It is possible that these principles of cell death, axonal competition, and modification of synaptic circuitry can be extended to other systems in the cortex. In a previous study we estimated that newborn

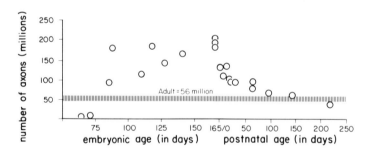

Figure 7.15
The estimated total number of axons in corpus callosum as a function of pre- and postnatal ages in postconceptual days. Each point represents a single animal. Error values (<14 percent) are smaller than or equal to the size of the dots used to represent each data point. The hatched line indicates the average total number of callosal axons in eight adult monkeys (from LaMantia and Rakic 1990).

monkeys lose over 70 percent of the axons within the hippocampal commissure as well as many axons within the anterior commissure (LaMantia and Rakic 1990). Clearly, the corpus callosum is not the only system of cortically projecting axons to show significant cell death, although we do not as yet understand the functional significance of these postnatal changes in cortical organization. In addition to axonal overproduction, there is also a considerable overproduction of synapses in the cortex (Rakic et al. 1986) (see figure 7.16). This overproduction occurs simultaneously in all major regions of the neocortex, and we speculated that this fact provides the possibility for competitive interaction.

In order to gauge the applicability of the competition model to the projections of cortical areas, an experiment was conducted in which partial occipital lobe removal was carried out in an embryonic rhesus monkey (Goldman-Rakic and Rakic 1984). The premise of this experiment was that neurons in the occipital and parietal lobes normally have partially overlapping projections early in development to at least some subcortical structures, such as the neostriatum, that normally become segregated later, presumably due to the effects of competition. In this experiment the monkey's brain was reexamined at 3 years of age. There was a striking enlargement in the inferior parietal lobules. These results have been replicated in an additional monkey. This result is further evidence that the competition model can be used to explain other aspects of the dynamics of cortical development besides the development of retino-geniculo-striate connections.

In a more speculative vein, we can imagine that in the course of evolution of a species, selection may have favored individuals with increased or decreased growth rates for one or more cortical areas. If a competition model is valid, it is entirely possible that additional changes in the structure of the brain could have occurred due to the effects of competition. For example, hypertrophy of some cortical areas in evolution may be related to the atrophy or reduction of importance of other areas.

Our experiments with eye enucleation provide an indirect test for this model by reducing the size of the thalamic input from the lateral geniculate nucleus to the primary visual cortex. The surgery has to be performed between E60 and E65, before photoreceptors could make any contacts with bipolar cells, and, most importantly, before layers IV, III and II in the cortex have been generated. In spite of this, the cortex developed a normal layering pattern, normal distribution of major neurotransmitter receptors, and synaptic density (Rakic 1988b; Rakic et al. 1987, 1991). However the total size of area 17 was much

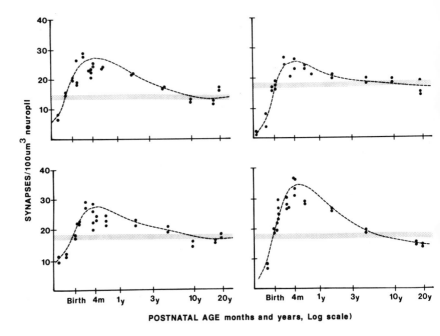

Figure 7.16
Histograms of the density of synapses per 100 square microns of neuropil in the primary somatosensory (A), primary motor (B), prefrontal (C), and primary visual (D) cortices at various ages. Each black dot represents the value obtained from an uninterrupted electron microscopic probe consisting of about 100 photographs across the entire depth of the cortex. The stippled horizontal stripe denotes the average synaptic density in the adult monkey for each area. Age in months (m) and years (y) is presented on a logarithmic scale in order to fit the entire span of the monkey onto a single graph (from Rakic et al. 1986).

smaller than in the control, indicating that thalamocortical afferents have considerable influence on the size of a given cortical area (Rakic 1988b).

In conclusion, we have learned that development of the cerebral cortex depends on the balance between genetically endowed properties and impact from the input from the periphery. As a result there is considerable plasticity in cortical development. This potential is normally hidden by the fact that development is a strongly canalized process in which major developmental targets are achieved if normal environmental stimulation is present. Nevertheless we can unmask this plasticity through the kinds of experiments I have described here. These experiments show that many aspects of cortical organization, including the sizes of cortical areas and some aspects of their connections, are determined by competition among an overabundance of neurons produced early in embryonic life (Rakic 1988b). We still know little about the mechanisms underlying these competitive processes; however, it is possible to study them experimentally and, in so doing, to learn more about the processes that influence the development of our marvellous organ of consciousness, the cerebral cortex.

References

Bourgeois, J. P., and Rakic, P. (1987). Distribution, density and ultrastructure of synapses in the visual cortex in monkeys devoid of retinal input from early embryonic stages. *Abst. Soc. Neurosci.* 13:1044.

Brodmann, K. (1909). Vergleichende Lokalisationslehre der Grosshirninde. Leipzig: Brath.

Cunningham, B. A., Hemperly, J. J., Murray, B. A., Prediger, E. A., Brackenbury, R., and Edelman, G. M. (1986). Neural cell adhesion molecule: structure, immunoglobin-like domains, cell surface modulation and alternating RNA splicing., *Science* 236:799–806.

Geschwind, N., and Galaburda, A. M. (1984). *Cerebral lateralization: Biological mechanisms, associations and pathology.* Cambridge: MIT Press.

Goldman-Rakic, P. S., and Rakic, P. (1984). Experimental modification of gyral patterns. In *Cerebral dominance: The biological foundation,* ed. N. Geschwind and A. M. Galaburda. 179–92, Cambridge: Harvard University Press.

Hatten, M. E., and Mason, C. A. (1986). Neuron-astroglia interactions *in vitro* and *in vivo. Trends in Neuroscience.* 9:168–74.

Hubel, D. H., and Wiesel, T. N. (1977). Ferrier lecture. Functional architecture of macaque monkey visual cortex. *PR* 198:1–59.

Hubel, D. H., Wiesel, T. N., and LeVay, S. (1977). Plasticity of ocular dominance columns in monkey striate cortex. *PT* 278:377–409.

Kuljis, R., and Rakic P. (1989). Multiple types of neuropeptide Y-containing neurons in primate neocortex. *J. Comp. Neurol.* 280(3):393–409.

LaMantia, A. S., and Rakic, P. (1990). Axon overproduction and elimination in the corpus callosum of the developing rhesus monkey. *Journal of Neuroscience,* 10(7):2156–75.

Levitt, P., Cooper, M. L., and Rakic, P. (1981). Coexistence of neuronal and glial precursor cells in the cerebral ventricular zone of the fetal monkey: An ultrastructural immunoperoxidase analysis. *J. Neurosci.* 1:27–39.

Livingstone, M. S., and Hubel, D. H. (1988). Segregation of form, color, movement, and depth: Anatomy, physiology and perception. *Science* 240:740–49.

Mason, C. A., and Hatton, M. E. (1985). How do growth cones grow? *Trends in Neuroscience* 8:304–6.

Otake, M. and Schull, W. J. (1984). In utero exposure of A-bomb radiation and mental retardation: A reassessment. *Br. J. Radiol.* 57.

Provis, J. M., van Driel, D., Billson, F. A., and Russell, P. (1985). Human fetal optic nerve: Overproduction and elimination of retinal axons during development. *J. Comp. Neurol.* 238:92–101.

Rakic, P. (1972). Mode of cell migration to the superficial layers of fetal monkey neocortex. *J. Comp. Neurol.* 145:61–84.

Rakic, P. (1974). Neurons in the monkey visual cortex: Systematic relation between time of origin and eventual disposition. *Science* 183:425–27.

Rakic, P. (1976). Prenatal genesis of connections subserving ocular dominance in the rhesus monkey. *Nature* 261:467–71.

Rakic, P. (1977). Prenatal development of the visual system in the rhesus monkey. *Phil. Trans. Roy. Soc. Lond. B.* 278:245–60.

Rakic, P. (1978). Neuronal migration and contact interaction in primate telencephalon. *Postgraduate Medical Journal* 54:25–40.

Rakic, P. (1981). Development of visual centers in the primate brain depends on binocular competition before birth. *Science* 214:928–31.

Rakic, P. (1983). Geniculo-cortical connections in primates: Normal and experimentally altered development. *Prog. Brain Res.* 58:393–404.

Rakic, P. (1985a). Limits of neurogenesis in primates. *Science* 227:154–56.

Rakic, P. (1985b). Contact regulation of neuronal migration. In *The Cell in Contact: Adhesions and Junctions as Morphogenetic Determinants,* ed. G. M. Edelman and J. -P. Thiery 67–91. New York: John Wiley & Sons.

Rakic, P. (1986). Mechanism of ocular dominance segregation in the lateral geniculate nucleus: competitive elimination hypothesis. *Trends in Neuroscience* 9:11–15.

Rakic, P. (1988a). Defects of neuronal migration and pathogenesis of cortical malformations. *Prog. Brain Res.* 73:15–37.

Rakic, P. (1988b). Specification of cerebral cortical areas. *Science* 241:170–76.

Rakic, P., Bourgeois, J. -P., Eckenhoff, M. E., Zecevic, N., and Goldman-Rakic, P. S. (1986). Concurrent overproduction of synapses in diverse regions of the primate cerebral cortex. *Science* 232: 232–35.

Rakic, P., Gallager, D., and Goldman-Rakic, P. S. (1988). Areal and laminar distribution of major neurotransmitter receptors in the monkey visual cortex. *J. Neurosci* 8:3670–90.

Rakic, P., and Goldman-Rakic, P. S. (1985). Use of fetal neurosurgery for experimental studies of structural and functional brain development in nonhuman primates. In *Perinatal Neurology and Neurosurgery,* ed. R. A. Thompson, J. R. Green, and S. D. Johnsen, pp. 1–15. New York: Spectrum.

Rakic, P., Kritzer, M., and Gallager, D. (1987). Distribution of major neurotransmitter receptors in the visual cortex of monkeys devoid of retinal input from early embryonic stages. *Abst. Soc. Neurosci.* 13:358.

Rakic, P., and Riley, K. P. (1983a). Regulation of axon numbers in the primate optic nerve by prenatal binocular competition. *Nature* 305:135–37.

Rakic, P., and Riley, K. P. (1983b). Overproduction and elimination of retinal axons in the fetal rhesus monkey. *Science* 209:1441–44.

Rakic, P., and Singer, W., eds. (1988). *Developmental neurobiology of neocortex.* New York: John Wiley & Sons.

Rakic, P., Suner, I., and Williams, R. (in press). A novel cytoarchitectonic area induced experimentally within the primate visual cortex. *Proceedings of National academy of Sciences (USA).*

Rakic, P., and Williams, R. W. (1986). Thalamic regulation of cortical parcellation: An experimental perturbation of the striate cortex in rhesus monkeys. *Abst. Soc. Neurosci.* 12:1499.

Schachner, E., Shani, J., Shechtman, M., and Pfeiffer, Y., (1985), Placental Transfer of Radioactive Salts In The Pregnant Rabbit. *International Journal of Nuclear Medicine and Biology,* 12(5):393–96.

Schmechel, D. E., and Rakic, P. (1979). A Golgi study of radial glial cells in developing monkey telencephalon. *Anat. Embryol.* 156:115–52.

Sidman, R. L., and Rakic, P. (1982). Development of the human central nervous system. In *Histology and histopathology of the nervous system,* ed. W. Haymeker and R. D. Adams, 3–145. C. C. Thomas.

Epilogue

Traditionally, developmental research has been guided by two overriding issues: continuity vs. discontinuity and nature vs. nurture. The first of these asks, How is development partitioned? The second asks, What is the source underlying the behaviors that we see developing in organisms? Although the chapters in this volume address both of these overriding issues, they focus attention on epigenesis and the role of genome-environment interaction. Thus although the nature-nurture issue has probably stimulated more empirical and theoretical work than any other issue in the field of developmental research, contemporary theorists have to a large degree redefined the issue.

Historically the nature-nurture issue has been conceptualized in at least three ways. The first, and now dated, conceptualization is that the innate mechanisms (the genetic component) underlying behavior are largely invariant and not affected by environmental stimuli. Instead of being variable, the innate mechanism is a rigid and immutable aspect of specific behavior. One might consider the onset of language development as one such example. Although onset itself is fixed, the amount and kind of environmental stimulation is clearly an important source of individual and cultural differences.

A second conceptualization, on the other hand, proffers that the innate mechanisms underlying behavior might best be conceptualized as varying among individuals. From this perspective, both heredity and environment are held to contribute to behavior, and the proportional contributions of each are not constant, but variable. The variability operates at both the population and the individual levels. The claim is that the particular genotype of an individual, while conferring structures, traits, and predispositions that an individual shares with some, but not all, subgroups, also endows the individual with the ability to respond to the environment in a unique way. In her chapter, Scarr shows that this conceptualization is inadequate to explain data on adoption and twinning.

The third conceptualization argues for change in plasticity over development. The idea is that "given a normal environment all members of a species will follow a fairly fixed course of development with little individual variation for the earliest stages of development" (Waterhouse 1983, 180). This relationship changes, however, as development proceeds, and increasingly the course of the individual development is determined by a set of complex interactions between environmental stimuli and genetic programs. In terms of this conceptualization, individual variations in behavior arise from epigenetic processes whose courses are both constrained and facilitated by genetic mechanisms (i. e., they are canalized).

The chapters in this volume are predicated on the assumptions of this third conceptualization. Kagan, for example, discusses the concept of continuity in development. Historically developmentalists have tended to exaggerate the importance of behavioral traits in childhood as predictors of adult behavior. Kagan points out, however, that recent research has shown that behaviors related to anxiety and the mitigation of anxiety have a strong biological base and show extraordinary continuity throughout an individual's life. He cites his own work on child development, including longitudinal and cross-cultural studies of both social behavior and psychophysiology (cardiac responding, skin resistance and EEG) to support his arguments. The concluding points of the chapter, however, make a different point. Although it now seems clear that the biological underpinnings of anxiety are strong, social factors can modify such behaviors substantially, and Kagan cites examples of how family socialization can change the overt behavior (although not the psychophysiological response) of individuals at both ends of the anxiety continuum.

Suomi's work on social development in rhesus monkeys closely parallels that of Kagan's with human children and provides additional evidence for, and insights into, socialization. The chapter describes important aspects of primate social behavior (including attachment behavior, parental behavior, and aggressiveness) and then goes on to show that important aspects of adult social behavior in monkeys can be predicted from traits exhibited in infancy. As is true in Kagan's work, continuity is most striking for behaviors associated with anxiety. Biochemical studies are also cited to show that individual differences related to anxiety reactions may be due to differences in the functioning of central monoamine neurons. This dovetails well with recent results in the field of psychopharmacology, showing that drugs manipulating these systems can have a strong influence on anxiety and depression. Suomi's work helps to explain the roles of both biological and social variables in personality characteristics among adults and their role in adaptability.

Scarr takes up the issue of social learning processes where Kagan and Suomi leave off. Focusing on family social interactions, Scarr shows that biological variables are also important and permanently shape the development of adult behavior. The effects of adoption and twinning are considered valuable for the light they shed on the sociocultural context of development. Adopting essentially an epigenetic frame, Scarr argues that children are active constructors of the contexts in which they develop (they both actively *select* and *elicit* those stimuli that direct their development). Scarr's chapter also focuses on the nature of developmental plasticity. She argues, quite persuasively, for the theory that as children mature, their behaviors become increasingly individuated since the experiences that modify their behavior are correlated with their genotypes.

Kuhl also considers the role of biological variables in human speech perception and language development. Human language provides one of the most elegant examples of the interaction of innate and environmental components in the development of complex behavior. As such, human language provides an example of canalized learning par excellence. Early investigators stressed the importance of cognitive specializations that underlie and guide speech perception and language development. Kuhl refines the role of biological preparedness for speech perception and language development through an ingenious series of comparative experiments on the perception of speech by human infants and by animals. Kuhl has found that much of the sophisticated ability for perceiving complex speech sound contrasts exhibited by preverbal human infants can also be observed in animals. These results argue for general biological mechanisms, probably common to a number of vertebrate auditory systems, playing an important role in guiding the earliest stages of speech perception and language acquisition in humans. Her results leave little need to postulate the existence of specialized processes unique to humans, dedicated to the processing of speech sounds, as the basis for the perception of basic speech sound categories.

On the other hand, she also cites work showing that human infants associate speech sounds with appropriate facial gestures used in production. These results argue convincingly for the existence of processes which are almost certainly uniquely human. This evidence for the existence of auditory-visual equivalence classes for speech sound in infants is but one indication of a host of sometimes subtle, yet powerful, innate predispositions to attend to and learn speech sounds in humans. Thus Kuhl's work points to the importance of biological preparedness based on interaction of basic biological mechanisms with species-specific predispositions in language learning. This model has parallels in the development of complex behaviors in other vertebrate systems as well.

Indeed, Marler reviews a comprehensive body of comparative data on song learning in birds that show striking parallels with the kinds of epigenetic processes hypothesized to underlie human language learning. Over the years, the study of vocal learning in birds has led to many important insights into the biopsychology of plasticity and learning. Included among these are the roles of brain lateralization, sexual dimorphism in brain structures, and hormonal influences in the acquisition of complex skilled behaviors. In developing his arguments, Marler cites his own work comparing song learning in two congeneric species of sparrows—the song sparrow and the swamp sparrow—as providing overwhelming evidence that vocal development is a strongly canalized process. Marler's work reveals a complicated, intricate system of motor proclivities, perceptual predispositions, and social influences that guide the vocal learning system during development. What emerges from these pages is a realization of the intimate nature of the relation between learning and instinct. It is for this reason that Marler has coined the phrase "instinct to learn" to describe song development in birds. Marler's comparative work is extremely important, not only for the insights it has already provided into the biology of learning but for the promise that the study of bird vocal learning holds for increasing our understanding of how neural mechanisms operate for these canalized processes.

The cerebral cortex is the organ of consciousness in mammals. As such, study of the factors controlling cortical development provides insights into the limits of developmental plasticity. Rakic details the methods and results of investigations aimed at elucidating cortical organization and ontogeny. He shows that there is extraordinary potential for plasticity in cortical development, which is normally masked by the fact that brain development is a highly canalized process. In discussing the nature of this plasticity, Rakic first describes his research elucidating the role of radial glial cells in cortical development, then shows that environmental conditions in the embryo guide the processes controlling both the size and organization of cortical areas. The basis for this is that an overabundance of neurons are produced during embryonic life many of which are not needed. These excess neurons are then eliminated by a process of competition and cell death in which incorrect or aberrant projections are removed. Aspects of this process continue after birth, with human infants losing up to 200 axons per second in the corpus callosum alone during the first weeks of early infancy. Rakic's work clearly implicates the role of epigenetic mechanisms in the development of neural circuits.

The work described in the chapters of this volume is path breaking and represents some of the most creative research being carried out in developmental biopsychology. Not only does this research address historically important issues in developmental research (continuity vs. discontinuity and nature vs. nurture), but it also provides a broader, unifying framework by focusing on epigenetic processes as tools for understanding the path of development both within and across species. Indeed the comparative frame characterizes many of the contributions contained in this volume and points to even more work to come using this method. These are exciting times for the field of developmental biopsychology. There is virtually an explosion of new data and theory in the neurosciences. The new output suggests that future directions will most certainly include analyses of both neural circuitry and cell mechanisms if we are to comprehensively understand developmental phenomena. Fortunately the possibilities are becoming realities with the methods that are increasingly available.

Recent developments in developmental psychology and related disciplines offer great promise for elucidating even further the core issues addressed in this volume. Three examples will illustrate this point. Current research in cognitive development is taking a closer look at Piaget's hypotheses about infant cognition, especially the sensorimotor stage of development.

Piaget (1951, 1952, 1954) claimed that thinking, in the sense of representation or symbolic functioning, emerges late in infancy (between 18 and 24 months). Prior to this time the infant's behavior is said to be more externally oriented. Current research on both perception and concept development (cf. Spelke 1988; Baillargeon 1987; Mandler 1990) presents a different picture of infant cognitive competence. The new findings indicate that infants have the ability to conceptualize at an earlier point in development than was theorized, especially by Piaget, to be the case (1951, 1952, 1954). The new findings have become possible largely because of the development of methods for investigating infant behavior that do not depend so heavily on the maturation of the motor system. One compelling piece of evidence for the presence of conceptual development is the infant's ability to demonstrate recall in the absence of both objects and events. New methods of investigation now show that between 9 and 11 months infants can imitate actions observed 24 hours earlier (cf. Meltzoff 1988; McDonough and Mandler 1989; Mandler 1990). Moreover, research by Baillargeon, De Vos, and Graber (1989) demonstrates that infants as young as 8 months of age can recall where objects were hidden after intervals lasting up to 70 seconds. These findings and the methods used to ascertain them argue well for the continued investigation by developmentalists of continuity-discontinuity, nature-nurture, and adaptability within and among species.

In the biological sciences, recent advances in molecular biology have pointed to important individual variations among humans despite considerable phenotypic similarities. Karlin, Kennett, and Bonne-Tamir (1979) report research displaying the use of heterogeneity indices and distance measures with respect to a standard. Employing both blood loci (HLA-A, HLA-B, ABO, MNSs, Rh, P, Duffy, and Kell) and protein loci (Acid phosphatase, adenylate kinase, adenosine deaminase, phosphoglucomutase, 6-Phosphogluconate dehydrogenase, and Haptoglobin), these investigators examined the correlation between morphological and anthropometric traits and biolchemical genetic constitution. Gene frequency data from different populations were used. The assumption underlying this research was that two populations can be related with respect to their allelic frequency arrays for sets of polymorphic genetic markers. Testing the assumption required the determination of a standard and the distance of each population from the standard for several genetic markers. Karlin, Kennett, and Bonne-Tamir (1979) found that there is not necessarily an isomorphism between general external body characteristics and underlying biochemistry. Some population groups that have similar external features have very different biochemical constituency and vice versa. Findings like these will greatly assist the cause of comparative research, as they offer the prospect of our gaining insight from the microlevel of functioning into issues of both phylogeny and ontogeny. This is precisely the kind of research that can provide insights into the mechanisms as well as the manifestations of canalization processes operating during development.

In considering these recent advances in two areas as seemingly disparate as developmental psychology and molecular biology, one cannot help but ponder how such advances might best be integrated. It is in just this domain that recent developments in artificial intelligence and computer science show a promise for major contributions. There have been exciting new attempts to describe a theory of brain function that can account for the most basic of behavioral phenomena—perceptual categorization and generalization (Edelman 1987). The essential problem is this: developing organisms face an unlabeled world in which environmental stimuli must be defined and categorized in order for individuals to learn to make effective decisions and adapt to changing environmental conditions. This problem presents a severe challenge to successful development of adaptive behavior. The recent theory of neuronal group selection provides one way of dealing with this problem (Edelman 1987; Changeaux and Konishi 1987). The view proffered by this theory is that differentiation and learning take place by selection of preexisting neurons, synapses, and even molecules. The selected neuronal connections, then, encode the relationship between stimulus and response necessary to categorize environmental stimuli. What is intriguing about this line of investigation based on neuronal selection, reentrant maps, and distributed systems is that such systems are readily modeled with existing computer technology. Although direct counterparts to the notion of canalization have not been developed, such applications would seem entirely appropriate since living systems that have successfully solved these problems appear to develop in this way.

The kinds of research described here may therefore provide new insights and tools for cognitive scientists by showing how real biological systems have evolved and how they function.

References

Baillargeon, R. (1987). Object permanence in 3.5 and 4.5 month-old infants. *Developmental Psychology* 23:655–64.

Baillargeon, R., De Vos, J., and Graber, M. (1989). Location memory in 8-month-old infants in a nonsearch AB task: Further evidence. *Cognitive Development* 4:345–67.

Changeaux, J. P., and Konishi, M. (1987). *The neural and molecular bases of learning.* New York: John Wiley & Sons.

Edelman, Gerald M. (1987). *Neural darwinism: The theory of neuronal group selection.* New York: Basic Books.

Karlin, Samuel, Kennett, R., and Bonne-Tamir, B. (1979). Analysis of biochemical genetic data on Jewish populations: II. Results and interpretations of heterogeneity indices and distance measures with respect to standards. *American Journal of Human Genetics* 31:341–65.

McDonough, L, and Mandler, J. M. (1989). Immediate and deferred imitation with 11-month-olds: A comparison between familiar and novel actions. Poster presented at meeting of the Society for Research In Child Development, Kansas City.

Mandler, J. M. (1990). A new perspective on Cognitive development in infancy. *American Scientist* 78:236–43.

Meltzoff, A. N. (1988). Infant imitation and memory: Nine-month-olds in immediate and deferred tests. *Child Development* 59:217–25.

Piaget, J. (1951). *Play, dreams and imitation in childhood.* New York: Norton.

Piaget, J. (1952). *The origins of intelligence in children.* New York: International Universities Press.

Piaget, J. (1954). *The construction of reality in the child.* New York: Basic Books.

Spelke, E. S. (1988). The origins of physical knowledge. In *Thought without language,* ed. L. Weiskrantz 168–84. New York: Clarendon Press.

Waterhouse, Lynn. (1983). *Individual variation in language acquisition,* Hiroshima, Japan: Bunka Hyoron Publishing Company.

Name Index

Abbs, J. H., 96, 102
Anderson, J. A., 73, 102
Anderson, J. R., 102
Ardell, L. H., 103
Aslin, R. N., 77, 102
Austin, G. A., 81, 102

Baah, J., 26
Baillargeon, R., 167, 169
Baker, M. C., 107, 124
Balaban, E., 113, 125
Bandura, A., 69, 70, 74
Baptista, L. F., 111, 115, 125
Barney, H. L., 84, 95, 105
Barsalou, L. W., 92, 104
Baysinger, C. M., 40, 41, 55
Bonne-Tamiv, B., 168, 169
Borton, R. W., 101, 105
Bouchard, T. J., 70, 71
Bourgeois, J. P., 155, 159
Bower, T. G. R., 101, 102
Bowlby, J., 12, 25, 41, 55
Bradley, R., 61, 70
Brazelton, T. B., 47, 55
Brodmann, K., 127, 140, 149, 159
Brown, S. D., 99, 102
Bruner, J. S., 81, 102
Burdick, C. K., 99, 102
Buss, D., 57, 70

Cairns, R., 13, 25
Caldwell, B., 61, 71
Carrell, T. D., 100, 105
Caspi, A., 69, 71
Changeaux, J. P., 169
Chomsky, N., 10, 73, 102
Clifton, R., 40, 56
Cohen, M. M., 93, 104
Cooper, F. S., 104

Cooper, M. L., 143, 159
Cronbach, L., 57, 71
Cronin, C., 55
Cummings, E. M., 15, 25
Cunningham, B. A., 145, 159
Cunningham, M. A., 107, 124

Darwin, C., 11
Defries, J., 65, 71
Dennis, A., 21, 25
De Vos, J., 167, 169
Diamond, A., 15, 25
Dittus, W. P. J., 37, 56
DiVirgilio, L., 13, 26
Dooling, R. J., 75, 99, 102, 105, 113, 125
Dunn, L. T., 24, 25

Edelman, G. M., 168, 169
Eimas, P. D., 76, 77, 101, 102
Elder, G. H., 69, 71
Ellis, H., 12, 25
Everitt, B. J., 24, 25

Fagan, J. F. III, 75, 102
Fant, G., 92, 99, 102
Fantz, R. L., 75, 102
Fellowes, J., 36, 56
Fernald, A., 75, 103
Fishbein, H. D., 6, 10
Fodor, J. A., 73, 74, 101, 103
Fu, C., 104
Fujimura, O., 105

Gans, S. J., 100, 105
Galaburda, A. M., 129, 159
Gallagher, D., 135, 160
Garcia-Coll, C., 18, 25
Gardner, B. T., 103
Gardner, R. A., 78, 103

Gelman, R., 26
Gersten, M., 18, 25, 26
Geschwind, N., 129, 159
Gibbons, J., 21, 26
Gleitman, H., 7, 10
Gleitman, L. P., 7, 10
Goldman-Rakic, P. S., 130, 135, 157, 159, 160
Goodnow, J. J., 81, 102
Gordon, J. W., 104
Gould, J. L., 108, 125
Grabe, M., 167, 169
Gracco, V. L., 96, 102
Graham, F., 40, 56
Grant, K. W., 93, 103
Green, K. P., 93, 100, 103, 104
Green, S., 103
Grieser, D. L., 75, 80, 88, 101, 103

Halle, 99
Hansen, E. W., 31, 56
Harlow, H. F., 30, 31, 34, 56
Harlow, M. K., 31, 34, 56
Harris, R. C., 13, 26
Hatter, M. E., 145, 159
Henker, B. A., 103
Hennessey, B. L., 102
Hen-Tov, A., 103
Higley, J. D., 56
Hinde, R. A., 21, 25
Hood, K. E., 13, 25
Hubel, D. H., 147, 148, 159
Hulse, S. H., 75, 102

Jakobson, 99
Jenkins, J. J., 105
Jusczyk, P., 102

Kagan, J., 3, 5, 13, 17–19, 21, 25, 26, 38, 56, 75, 103, 164, 165
Karlin, S., 168, 169
Kearsley, R., 19, 26
Kelly, W. J., 105
Kennett, R., 168, 169
Kessen, W., 96, 97, 103
Klein, R. E., 77, 104
Konishi, M., 117, 118, 125, 169
Kroodsma, D. E., 118, 125
Kuhl, P. K., 3, 7, 8, 9, 74, 75, 78–80, 84, 88–90, 93–97, 99–101, 104, 165

LaMantia, A. S., 156, 157, 159
Lasky, R. E., 77, 104
Lenneberg, E. H., 7, 10
LeVay, S., 148, 159
Levine, J., 96, 103
Levitt, D., 143, 159
Lewis, M., 103
Liberman, A. M., 73, 74, 76, 104
Lieberman, P., 78, 96, 101, 104
Lightfoot, D., 7, 10
Loehlin, J. C., 65, 71
Lorenz, K. S., 108, 124, 125
Lykken, D. T., 64, 71

McClelland, J. L., 73, 105
Maccoby, E. E., 36, 56
MacDonald, J., 93, 104
McDonough, L., 167, 169
McGurk, H., 93, 104
MacKain, K., 95, 104
Magruder, T. V., 69, 71
Mandler, J., 167, 169
Marler, P., 2, 3, 8, 9, 108, 109, 111, 115, 117, 118, 120, 121, 125, 166
Martin, C. S., 86, 105
Mason, C. A., 145, 160
Mason, W. A., 15, 26
Massaro, D. W., 93, 104
Mattingly, A. P., 19, 26
Mattingly, I., 73, 74, 101, 104
Mayr, E., 57, 71
Medin, D. L., 92, 104
Meltzoff, A. N., 75, 80, 95–97, 99, 101, 104, 105, 167, 169
Miller, J. L., 105
Miller, J. T., 78, 93, 99, 100, 102–105
Miyawaki, K., 76, 105
Moore, M. K., 75, 101, 105
Moos, R. H., 61, 71
Moss, B. S., 61, 71
Moss, H. A., 12, 13, 19, 26
Mullenix, J. W., 86, 105
Myer, K. K., 13, 26

Newman, E. B., 106
Newport, E., 7, 10
Northcutt, R. G., 9, 10

Ohman, L. E., 55
Olweus, D., 13, 26
Otake, M., 145, 160

Padden, D. M., 78, 104
Papousek, H., 96, 105
Papousek, M., 105
Pastore, R. E., 105
Patterson, G. R., 69, 71
Perey, A. J., 102
Peters, S., 111, 118, 120, 121, 125
Peterson, G. E., 84, 95, 105
Petitto, L. A., 16, 26
Petrinovich, L., 111, 115, 125
Piaget, J., 96, 105, 167, 169
Pickert, R., 113, 125
Pisoni, D. B., 86, 100, 102, 105
Plomin, R., 62, 65, 71

Radke-Yarrow, M., 15, 25
Rakic, P., 2, 3, 8, 9, 130, 135, 137, 138,
    140, 142–150, 152, 154–161, 166, 167
Rasmussen, K. L. R., 36, 56
Rathbun, C., 13, 26
Redican, W. K., 56
Reznick, J. S., 17, 18, 21, 25, 26, 38, 56
Riley, K. P., 152, 160
Rosch, E., 88, 92, 105
Rosenberg, A., 26
Rummelhardt, D. E., 73, 105

Samuel, A. G., 88, 105
Sanford, D. L., 104
Scanlan, J. M., 41, 43, 48, 56
Scarr, S., 3, 6, 63, 71, 163, 165
Schachner, E., 145, 161
Schmechel, D. E., 143, 161
Schneider, M. L., 47, 56
Searcy, M. H., 125
Searcy, W. A., 113, 117, 125
Seay, B. M., 31, 56
Shankweiler, D. P., 104
Sheldon, W. H., 19, 26
Shell, W. J., 145, 160
Sherman, V., 115, 117, 125
Sidman, R. L., 145, 161
Simon, T., 75, 103
Siqueland, E. R., 102
Snideman, N., 38, 56
Snidman, N., 17, 26
Sparks, D. W., 103
Spelke, E., 26, 167, 169
Spieker, S., 104
Starkey, P., 11, 26
Stern, D., 104

Stern, W., 11, 26
Stevens, K. N., 89, 91, 105
Stevens, S. S., 106
Strange, W., 105
Streeter, L. A., 77, 106
Studdert-Kennedy, M., 96, 104, 106
Summerfield, Q., 93, 106
Suomi, S. J., 3, 5, 9, 30, 33, 34, 36, 42, 48,
    49, 53, 55, 56, 165
Sussman, E. J., 12, 26
Syrdal-Lasky, A., 77, 104

Tellegen, A., 64, 71
Tinbergen, N., 108, 124, 125
Turvey, M. T., 74, 104

Verbrugge, R., 105
Vigorito, J., 102
Volaitis, L. E., 88, 105
Volkman, J., 106

Waddington, C. H., 1, 10
Waldfogel, S., 13, 26
Waterhouse, L., 164, 169
Weinberg, R., 62, 63, 71
Wendrich, K. A., 96, 103
Wier, C. C., 105
Wiesel, T. N., 147, 148, 159
Williams, R., 154, 161
Winick, M., 13, 26

Zahn-Waxler, C., 15, 25
Zelazo, P., 19, 26

Subject Index

Academic ability, 13
Acquisition phase (of song learning), 121
ACTH, 39, 42, 43
Adaptability, 16
Adaptive behaviors, 34
Adaptive significance, 3
  of epigenetic programs, 6
Adolescence, 43, 44
  in monkeys, 44, 45
Adoptee's family members, 60
Adoption, 6
  adopted siblings, 63, 67
  and twinning, 165
Adrenergic receptors, 131, 135
Adrenocortical output, 5
Afferent connections, 147
Afferent projections, 132
Age-mate friendships, 33, 36
Aggressive children, 69
Aggressivity, 13
All-male gangs (primates), 36
Amygdala, 21, 23
Anterior commisure, 157
Antidepressant, 55
  compounds, 42
  imipramine hydrochloride, 45
Anxiety, 27,46, 60
Anxiety-producing situations, 5
Anxiety scores, 60
Anxiolytic compounds, 55
Area 17, 130, 147, 150, 152, 157. See also
  Striate cortex
Arterial tree, 22
Artificial intelligence, 168
Attachment behavior, 164
Auditory-articulatory mapping rules, 96
Auditory templates, 118
  for song, 115

Auditory-visual cross-modal perception,
  80
Auditory-visual equivalence classes, 165
Auditory-visual equivalents for speech,
  96
Auditory-visual speech perception, 101
Autoradiograms, 138, 149
Autoradiography, 136
Axon
  competition, 149, 156
  degeneration, 152
  elimination, 150, 156
  overproduction, 157
  projections, 132, 133
  rearrangement, 149

Behavioral
  characteristics, 1, 5
  inhibition, 20, 21, 47
  interactions, 62
  and morphological phenotypes, 3
  styles, 18
  traits, 27
Behaviorally based interventions, 28
Behaviorally reactive individuals, 39
Biobehavioral responses, 43
Biological
  factors in development, 5
  preparedness, 7
  relatives, 62
  siblings, 6, 68
  signals in development, 3, 6
  twins, 6. See also Twins
Biology of human language, 74
Brain lateralization, 166
Brain maturation, 15
Breeding colony, 37
Breeding populations, 2

Cajal impregnation, 130
Canalization, 2, 57, 159, 164, 166, 168–169
 mechanisms, 8
Canalized learning, 165
Canalized process, 6
Canaries, 121
Canonical babbling, 76
Cardiac conditioning response, 43
Cardiac function, 39
Cardiac responding, skin resistance, and EEG, 164
Cardiac response, 41
 patterns, 5
Cardio-vascular functioning, 22
Caretaking skills, 30
Catecholamine, 42, 45
Catecholamine turnover, 43. See also Norepinephrine
Categorical perception, 7, 70, 76, 79, 86, 99, 100–101
 in animals, 78
 in chinchillas, 78
 in infants and children, 79
 and linguistic environment, 76
 in monkeys, 78
Cell death, 152, 156–157
 and competition, 152, 155, 157, 159
Cell migration, 154
Cellular mechanisms, 127
Cerebral cortex, 2, 127, 159, 166
Chemoarchitecture, 155
Childhood, 43
Child's IQ, 60, 69. See also IQ
Cingulate gyrus, 141
CNS norepinephrine turnover, 49
Cognitive competence, 167
Cognitive functions, 2
Communication, 73
Comparative
 approach, 3, 7
 frames, 167
 psychologist, 3
 research (method and strategy), 74, 166, 168
 studies, 124
 studies of speech perception, 78
Competition, 152, 155, 157, 159, 166
 and cell death, 166
 lack of, 150

Competitive processes in brain development, 159
Competitors, 37
Computer generated speech sounds, 76, 84
Computer technology, 169
Conceptual development, 167
Conspecific song, 111, 113, 115,
 preferences, 111
 syntax, 115
Contact comfort, 30
Continuity, 3–168
 in development, 3, 5, 6, 12–14, 74, 164
 and discontinuity, 11, 163, 167–168
 of emotions, 12
 hypothesis (of speech evolution), 79
Coping strategies, 5
Corpus callosum, 132, 146, 156–157
Corpus striatum, 21
Cortex, 2, 129, 148, 157
Cortical areas for speech and language, 129
Cortical circuitry
 pattern of, 8, 131, 167
 in primates, 2
Cortical connectivity, 130
 columnar organization, 146
 columns, 154
 development, 141, 166
 layer, 130, 145
 malformation, 145
 maps, 127
 migration, 145
 morphogenesis, 143
 neurogenesis, 141, 143
 ontogeny, 8
 organization, 130, 159, 166
Cortices, 158
Corticotropin-releasing hormone, 24
Cortisol, 22, 43
 elevations, 43
 values, 22
Cross-fostering studies, 5, 48
Cross-modal correspondence classes for speech sounds in infants, 100
Cross-modal equivalence
 in infants, 94
 for speech sounds, 93
Cross-modal perception, 93, 97, 99
 in infants, 95

in speech, 80
Cross-modal relations between touch
  and vision, 101
Cross-sectional samples, 16
Crystallized song, 118–121
CSF, 44–46
  levels of catecholamine, 44
  MHPG levels, 45–46
  norephenephrine levels, 46
Cytoarchitecture, 127, 135, 145
  of cortical areas, 147
  of cortical fields, 129, 147

Deafness
  in children, 16
  in parents, 16
Dependency, 13
Depressive, 27, 42
  disorders, 27
  reactions, 42
Developmental, 3–43
  biopsychology, 3
  processes, 5
  shift, 43
Diastolic blood pressure, 22
Discontinuity (in development), 13–14,
  16
Distress vocalizations, 15
Distributed neural machinery, 73
Distributed systems, 169
Dizygotic twins, 19, 67–68
  correlations, 63
Dominance hierarchy, 28, 55
Dorsal lateral geniculate nucleus (LGd),
  155. See also LGd, lateral geniculate

Ectomorphic, 19
Ectopic projections, 8
Efferent connections, 147
Electron microscopy, 143
Embryogenesis, 140
Embryonic, 129–147
  development, 141
  forebrain, 146
  life, 129
  rhesus monkey, 147
Empathy, 15–16
Enabling signals, 115
Endocrine functions, 39
Enhance development, 68

Enucleation, 147, 152–153, 154–155
  bilateral, 154–155
Environmental
  factors, 57
  novelty and challenge, 27
  signals, 1, 3, 6
  stimulation, 3
  stimuli, 164
Epigenesis, 1, 4–6, 8, 58, 65, 70, 163
Epigenetic, 1, 58, 165
  interaction, 66
  mechanisms, 167
  processes, 2–3, 6, 70, 164, 166–167
  programs, 3, 5–6, 66
  systems, 1, 3
Esophageal tubes, 41
Evocative experiences, 66–67
Evolution, 3, 11, 129, 157
  of language, 73–74
  of speech, 100
Evolutionary theory, 11, 57
Exploratory behavior in monkeys, 49
Exposure to novelty, 39
Extra-striate cortex, 153
Eysenck personality inventory, 60

Families
  correspondence in, 41
  environment of, 61
  social interactions in, 165
Fearful, 37, 42
Feral environment, 36
Fetal brain, 139, 141
5HIAA (5–hydroxy-indoleacetic acid), 46
5–HT, 136. See also Serotonin
Flycatchers, 118
Forced monogamy, 30
Formant frequency, 82
Foster grandparents (in monkeys), 53
Fraternal twins, 6, 63, 67–68. See also
  Twins
Full siblings, 41

Gamma aminobuteric acid (GABA), 133
Gender-specific play activities, 36
Gene-environment interactions, 62
Genes, 2–3
Genetic, 163
  endowment, 107, 159
  factors, 57

Genetic (cont.)
  predisposition, 70, 108–109
  programs, 1–3, 164
  similarity, 67
  variability, 64
  variation, 64
Geniculate body, 147. *See also* Lateral geniculate; Dorsal lateral geniculate nucleus
Geniculo-striate visual pathway, 8
Genome, 1, 8
  environment interaction, 163
Genotype, 1, 4, 16, 20, 163, 165
Geographical isolation, 2
Germinal cells, 146
Golgi
  impregnations, 131
  methods, 130
  stain, 143

Heart rates, 15
  changes, 41
  conditioning, 40
  decreases in, 40
  levels, 38
Heritability, 19
  coefficients, 41
Heterogeneity indices, 168
Heterospecific songs, 111, 113, 115
Higher-order cognitive functions, 73
High-reactive
  biological parents, 49
  monkeys, 38, 49,
  pedigree, 53, 55
Hippocampal commisure, 157
Hiroshima, 145
Histochemistry, 129
Home environment, 6, 61–62, 64
Home scale, 61
Homologous, 5
  processes, 9
Homoplasy, 9
Hormonal influences, 166
Horseradish peroxidase (HRP), 132
Huddling behavior, 42
Humans
  language of, 73, 166
  neonatal exams of, 47
  reactive depression in, 42
  species-typical program of, 65
  speech perception of, 165

HVA (Homovanillic acid), 46
Hybrid syllable (song), 116
Hyperactive, 43
Hyperaggressive, 34
Hypertrophy, 8
Hypothalamic-pituitary-adrenal axis, 21–22
  activity, 42
Hypothalamus, 21, 24

Identical twins, 63, 67. *See also* Twins
Imipramine, 45–46
Imitation
  of facial actions, 75
  by songbirds, 120
Immunocytochemistry, 129
Immunohistochemical
  methods, 135, 143
  techniques, 133
Index
  of inhibition, 18
  of physiological activity, 22
Individual
  characteristics, 58
  differences, 27, 48
  organisms, 1
  variation, 1
Individual variability, 57
  in intelligence, 63
Indoleamine metabolites, 44
Infancy, 5, 11, 12, 38
Infant
  cognition, 167
  exploratory behavior, 32
  pedigree, 49
Inhibited, 17–19, 20–23
  behavior, 20, 24
  children, 24
Innate predispositions, 165
Innate release mechanism, 108–109
Input from the periphery, 159
In situ hybridization, 129
Instinct, 107, 109, 121
  to learn, 2, 108
Instinctive behavior, 113
Intellectual and personality development, 5, 58
Interaction with peers, 38
Intervention fallacy, 62
Introversion-extroversion, 60

IQ
  average, 68
  child's, 60–69
  and personality test scores, 64
  test scores, 6, 60, 63–64
Irritability, 16

Juvenile period (in monkeys), 33

Laid-back monkeys, 38–39, 41
Laminar organization (of the cortex), 154
Language
  abilities, 73
  development, 165
  evaluation, 74
  modularization, 73
  signals, 73
Larynx, 22
Lateral geniculate, 133, 152. *See also* LGd
  layers, 150
  nuclei, 150, 152–153
  of the thalamic, 147
Lateral migration, 146
Learning, 107–109, 166
  dialects (songbirds), 115, 122
  disability, 13
  preferences, 115
  processes, 2, 113
  songs, 122
Levels of plasma cortisol, 49
LGd, 154. *See also* Lateral geniculate
Life span, 1, 5
Ligand-binding techniques, 135
Limbic system, 21
  cortex, 141
Locomotion (in monkeys), 49
  skills, 31
Longitudinal research
  samples, 16
  studies, 13
Low-reactive pedigrees (in monkeys), 49

Macaque social groups, 28
Macaque troops, 55
Macroenvironmental events, 69
Male and female rhesus monkeys, 36–37
Maternal half siblings, 41
Maternally reared monkeys, 44
Maternal style, 48
Matriarchal
  kinship, 28

lineages, 28
lines, 29
Maturation, 14
Mature song, 118, 120
Mechanisms, 5
  of canalization, 1
Mel scale, 89
Memory, 2
Mesomorphic, 19
MHPG, 42, 44
Microenvironments, 69
Migration of neuroblasts, 2, 146
Mitotic figure, 141–142
Modification of synaptic circuitry, 156
Modularized system, 74
Module, 73
Monoamine neurons, 164
Monoclonal antibody, 143
Monozygotic twins, 19, 67–68. *See also*
  Twins
  IQ correlations, 63
Motherese, 75
Mother-infant interactions, 33
Mothering styles, 55
Motor
  activity, 16
  development, 118
Multigenerational matriarchal kinship
  lines, 28, 37
Multiple peer friendships, 37
Muscle tension, 22

Natal
  groups, 36–37
  troop, 28, 36
Natural psychological boundaries, 79
Natural selection, 3, 11, 157
Nature and nurture, 11, 163, 167–
  168
Neonatal
  measures, 49
  test score, 49
Neural basis (of behavior), 2
Neural network, 73
Neuroanatomical techniques, 129
Neuroblasts, 143
  migration, 141, 143
Neurogenesis, 2, 137, 139
Neuronal
  connectivity, 2
  formation, 129

Neuronal (cont.)
  group selection, 169
  interconnections, 2
Neurons
  overabundance of, 159
Neuropeptide Y, 133, 134, 139
Neuroticism, 60
Neurotransmitters, 5, 44–45, 133, 157
Noradregenic neural networks, 46
Norepinephrine, 24, 44, 46
  metabolite (MHPG), 42, 44
Normal layering pattern, 157
Nursery reared, 41
Nurturance, 48, 55
Nurturing
  foster mother, 53
  style, 53

Occipital lobe, 154
Ocular dominance, 147, 149
  columns, 148, 150, 152
Ontogenetic
  adaptation, 12
  columns, 144, 146–147, 154–155
  mechanisms, 3
  processes, 2, 115
  programs, 3, 107
Ontogeny, 5, 11
  of language, 74
  social-behavioral, 37
Oscine songbirds, 2, 8, 118

Parental
  behavior, 164
  love and control, 62
Parent's IQ scores, 60. See also IQ
Parietal lobes, 8
Parturition, 37
Paternal half siblings, 41
Peer interactions, 33–34
Perception, 2
Perceptual categorization and generalization, 168
Period of breeding, 33
Peripheral signals, 149
Personality characteristics, 5, 27, 60
Pharmacological interventions, 28
Phenotype, 1, 3–5, 16
  characteristics, 2
  patterns, 9
Phonetic

boundaries, 79
categorization, 84
category, 79, 84
Phonology of song syllables, 111
Phylogeny and ontogeny, 168
Physical exploration, 40
Physiological
  correlates, 5
  measures, 43
  responses, 5
Piaget's hypotheses, 167
Placebo treatment, 45
Planum temporale, 129
Plasma cortisol, 39, 42
  levels, 43
Plasticity, 166
Plastic song, 118–121
Play (in monkeys)
  patterns, 34
  situation, 40
Population approaches, 57
Predators, 37
Predispositions, 5, 163
  to react, 117
Predominant state, 47
Prepared learning, 75
Primary motor cortices, 158
Primary visual cortex, 130, 158
Primate
  cerebral cortex, 2
  social behavior, 164
Projection patterns (of cortical neurons), 132
Proliferative, 144
  region, 146
  units, 142, 144
  zones, 143, 146
Proprietary instinct, 12
Protomap, 147
Prototype
  effect, 93, 99
  hypothesis, 90
  theory, 92
Proximal, 58
Proximate causal sequences, 1–4
Psychophysiology, 164
Puberty, 36
Pupilary dilation, 22
Pyramidal
  cells, 131
  neurons, 132

Radial glia, 145–146
  cells, 143, 166
  fibers, 144
Reactive individuals, 39
Recall, 167
  memory, 14–15
Receptors, 24, 133, 155
  for neurotransmitters, 131, 137
  for opioids, 24
  sites, 135
Red-winged blackbird, 123, 124
Reentrant maps, 169
Relaxed monkeys (laid-back), 38
Releaser, 108
Reproductive behavior, 2
Resonant frequency (for speech), 82
Response to novelty (among monkeys),
  39
Retino-geniculo-striate connections, 157
Retrograde intra-axonal transport, 133
Rhesus monkeys, 5, 27–29, 31, 34, 36,
  39–40, 43–44, 127, 149
  adolescents, 33
  infants, 30, 33, 47–48
  juveniles, 36
Rough and tumble (among monkeys)
  activities, 36
  play, 36

Same-sex subgroups, 34
Selection, 4
Self-directed behavior, 49
Semi-wild environments, 36
Sensitive period, 108, 121–122, 124
  for learning, 121
Sensorimotor stage, 167
Separation, 42
  anxiety, 15
  fear, 15
Serotonin, 44, 136
  receptors, 131, 135, 155
Sexual dimorphism, 166
Shyness, 20
  in children, 20
  in monkeys, 37
Sign language, 16
Sign stimuli, 108–109, 115
Skeletal motor system, 21
Sleeping patterns, 42
Smiling, 16
Sociability, 20

Social
  behavior, 2
  development, 27, 164
  fear, 5
  play, 36
  relationships (among monkeys), 42, 53
Socialization, 164
Somatosensory, 158
Song
  development, 123
  learning, 8, 109, 111, 115, 124, 166
  phrases, 123
  sparrows, 109–117, 123, 166
  stimulation, 118
  syllables, 112, 114–115, 123
  syntax, 109, 115, 123
  templates, 118
  types, 123
Songbird, 107, 122
  dialects, 107
Sound spectogram, 110
Spatio-temporal pattern, 2
Special mechanisms hypothesis (of
  speech evolution), 101
Speciation, 1
Species, 1–2
  characteristics, 58, 65
  features, 57
  normative developmental declines, 49
  specific vocalizations, 2
  typical (pattern), 30
  typical (processes), 1, 8
Species-specific
  biases, 124
  predispositions, 124, 166
  stimulus, 117
Speech
  development of, 101
  in infants, 80, 82
  and language, 73
  modules, 74
  perception, 6, 74
  production, 74
  sound categorization, 81, 85–88, 101
  sound generalization, 90
  sound perception, 99–100
  sound prototypes, 80, 88–93, 99, 101
  stimuli-processing mechanisms, 101
Stereotypy (emergence of), 43
Stimulus generalization, 90
Striate cortex, 152–154

Strongly canalized, 1
Sublayers, 148
Subsong, 118–119, 121
Subventricular zone, 142
Swamp sparrows, 109–117, 119–121, 166
Sympathetic nervous system, 21
Sympathetic tone, 22
Synapses, 157
  density, 155, 157–158
  overproduction in the cortex, 157
Syntactical features of song, 111–112
Synthetic songs, 123

Talker normalization, 80–82, 87, 99
  for computer-generated speech sounds,
    84
  in infants, 80, 82, 86
  for vowel sounds, 81
Temperament, 16
Temperamentally inhibited children, 25
Temperamental qualities, 16
Template system, 118
Teratogens, 141, 145
Thalamocortical afferents, 159
Thought, 2
[3H] thymidine, 137–138, 140
3–methoxy–4–hydroxy phenyleneglycol
  (MHPG), 42
Threshold of reactivity, 24
Toddler stage, 31
Topographic organization, 152
Traits, 5
Tritiated thymidine, 137, 139
Troops (of monkeys), 28, 36–37
Twins, 6
  biological, 6
  dizygotic, 19, 67–68
  identical, 63, 67
  monozygotic, 19, 63, 67–68
Typological approaches, 57

Ultimate causal sequence, 1–4
Uninhibited children, 17–18, 20–23
Universal law, 57
Uptight monkeys, 38–39, 41–42

Variation in intelligence, 64
Ventral
  contact (in monkeys), 49, 53
  pallidum, 23

striatum, 23
surface, 30
Ventricular
  layer, 146
  zone, 142, 144
Visual and auditory events, 23
Visual cortex, 147, 149–150, 152, 155
Visual thalamus, 150
Vocal communication, 75
Vocal cords, 22
Vocal imitation, 97, 99, 101
  in birds, 166
  in infants, 80, 96–98
  learning, 2
  perturbation, 22
Voice quality, 22
Vowel prototypes (from different lan-
  guages), 92

Wechsler adult intelligence scale, 58
  IQ scores, 60, 63
Withdrawn monkeys, 42–43

X-ray irradiation, 145

Young adulthood (in monkeys), 37